What Others Are Saying

"I can only say that Mo has written **a must-read gem**. He combines spirituality with science to explore deep truth that will resonate with hungry hearts and inquiring minds. He unwinds it all on a **personal revelatory trip into areas of truth laid out and explained in ways I have never read before**. From the dawn of creation to the awakening of your true self, Mo unpacks insights that can only come through revelation from the depths of the Christ.

His **takeaways at the end of each chapter are rich**, and ties together all that you have just read. They are spot on theologically, and gave me pause to reflect on what I had just read and on what I believe. I found that once I started reading, I **could not put the book down**... I think you will experience this also as you journey *Into the Abyss*, and discover for yourself the depths of the eternal Christ. It is just under 200 pages of great reading, and I highly recommend it."

Pastor Don Keathley, Houston, TX
President, Don Keathley Ministries
President, Global Grace Seminary

"It takes a brilliant and creative mind to be able to take complex ideas, such as what we see in the science of astronomy, and break it down into bite-size pieces in writing for the non-scientific mind. Mo does this very effectively! I especially appreciate his ability to show the **interconnection between science and theology**, which is desperately needed in today's world of rampant fundamentalism. For anyone with an open mind and open heart, this book **will be a combined feast** of the best of science blended with the best of theology."

Pastor Jim Peyton, Frog Jump, TN

"In his book *Into the Abyss*, Mo Thomas has created a **clear, concise communication of the cosmic correlation of Christ**. A read well invested!"

Bob Ingle, Lawrence, KS

"*Into the Abyss* by Mo Thomas is a wonderful pulling together of **science, faith, knowledge, dreams, thoughts, and personal experience** which retells the Jesus Story outside of its western shackles. The first thing that occurred to me in reading it was the compelling similarity to my own experience of leaving institutional religion, and beginning to search for the Jesus who was masked and silenced by our collective blindness. *Into the Abyss* will be **greatly valued as a trail map** of deconstruction, and into the great beyond."

Wendy and Don Francisco, Fort Collins, CO

"**Into the Abyss grabbed our hearts** and left us wanting more. It's easy to read and drew us in immediately. In a few words, it is...**beautiful, honest, sincere, vulnerable, real, tantalizing, drawing, appetizing, and intriguing**. We're honored to have had a "behind the scenes" peek into this beautiful life story, and call the author our friend!! Tears are streaming down our faces as we realize all that is coming to fruition in our lives. **This book will cause "soul-quakes" around the world**, and give people permission to explore the possibilities...to rise up from the ashes and live from their true Reality - their true Source."

Dave and Kay Carringer, Cleveland, TN

"Mo's writing is **exquisite, vulnerable**, and beautifully presents the **compelling Mystery of Christ** that longs to include us in the Dance."

Brian Longridge, Kerala, India

"*Into the Abyss* is a **delightful and mind-melting read**. And more than that, it's a **big, shiny wrecking ball that demolishes two of the main strongholds** that hold people back from the freedom available to them in Christ: Gnosticism and legalism. In regard to Gnosticism, with its dismissal of the physical world, **such philosophy is blown to pieces** as we discover just how much our creation is linked with the eternal realms of glory. As for legalism, the portrait of the Divine contained in this book leaves no place for the guilt/fear models of theology to hide. It **banishes them at the speed of light**! Dive in deep!"

Nick Padovani, West Milford, NJ
Author of The Song of the Ages
Lead Pastor at The Almond Branch

"**I recently asked Abba to help me remember** when I knew Them before the foundation of the world. Little did I know They would answer my prayer when "out of the blue" Mo invited me to proofread his book! **I was quickly drawn in at the beginning** as he described his black hole experience, and what it was like on the other side. I was captivated as he described Their incredible Beauty, and how he was overwhelmed by Their intense Love! Reading his journey, and **understanding how quantum physics validates the reality of Christ has significantly strengthened my faith**, elevating my awareness of our oneness with Them in perfect Love. I trust you will also be blessed by reading his story!"

Juliah Bornick, Madison, WI

INTO THE ABYSS

Discover Your True Identity in the
Infinite Depths of Christ

Copyright © 2020 by Mo Thomas
Into the Abyss
by Mo Thomas

Published by Eyes Open Press
www.eyesopenpress.com

All rights reserved solely by the author. The author guarantees all contents are original and do not infringe upon the legal rights of any other person or work. No part of this book may be reproduced in any form without the permission of the author.

Scripture quotations taken from the Amplified Bible, Classic Edition (AMPC). Copyright © 1954, 1958, 1962, 1964, 1965, 1987 by The Lockman Foundation. Used by permission. All rights reserved.

Scripture quotations taken from the New American Standard Bible (NASB). Copyright © 1960, 1962, 1968, 1971, 1972, 1973, 1975, 1977, 1995 by The Lockman Foundation. Used by permission. All rights reserved.

Scripture quotations taken from the New Living Translation (NLT). Copyright © 1996, 2004, 2015 by Tyndale House Foundation. Used by permission of Tyndale House Publishers Inc., Carol Stream, Illinois 60188. All rights reserved.

Scripture quotations taken from The Voice™ (VOICE). Copyright © 2008 by Ecclesia Bible Society. Used by permission. All rights reserved.

Cover Design & Art by Matt McClay

ISBN-13: 978-0-9991806-6-2 (paperback)

ISBN-13: 978-0-9991806-7-9 (e-book)

Printed in the United States of America

Thank You!

Sherry Thank you for the space you've given for me to take the time to write. A lot of the deeper questions that frame this book came from versions of things you asked in our early interactions about God and spirituality... I'm grateful.

Daniel and Delani You both bring me more joy than you could ever know. Thank you for teaching this old man about childlikeness and about what God is really like, past all the religious baggage I carried and sometimes still do. You are and will always be my greatest treasures.

Bill Napoleone A good portion of this material came from our whiteboards and our pizza times together, so you should recognize just about everything in here! I look forward to enjoying Chicago-style deep dish and Frozen Dew together with you in the future kingdom. And to the peeps by the pond: a better US and a better U.S., under future president Fields!

Dave and Kay Carringer I cannot begin to tell you how much of an encouragement you both have been to me, from opening your home and hearts these past several years, to your constant gifts of love and kindness through the wormhole. I treasure you with all my heart. Love to all our friends at Lion's Gate!

Biyi Akinlude I was supposedly the mentor when we first met, but somehow over the years the script has flipped and you started teaching me. Thank you for your passion, your creativity, and your steady affirmations for so many years. You have what it takes to change the world...Biyi Light, NHB.

Sarah Jackson and the EMU whiteboard crew When you asked Bill and I and the marketplace folks to start coming down and sharing with the EMU students, who could have known the gift that those years would become for all of us. What a joy to see you foster such an open, humble posture before God that allowed ALL of us to participate in what the Spirit was showing. Thank you.

Rick Kaatz Somehow, you believed in what I was doing before you had any idea about the content, and I will be eternally grateful for you seeing something before you saw anything. Your investment in me meant the world, and exemplifies the kind of generosity that I hope will mark my own life.

Binu Jacob and Tom VanGaalen Though separated by many miles, the space we've shared for so many years has been a treasure and an inspiration to help frame and rethink a lot of content that ended up in this book. Thank you for the gift of your friendship. Masala dosa is next on the agenda for sure!

Matt McClay The cover art is better than I could have hoped, and simply but beautifully captures the essence of what I am trying to convey. It also carries the whimsical, childlike flavor of my all-time favorite book—*The Little Prince*... What a gift this was, and you are, to me. Thank you!

Nick Padovani Wow. Somehow, you were able to get behind my eyes and into my heart, diving into the details to help this manuscript flow, while allowing me to keep my "voice." This is no easy task!! I'm so grateful for your friendship over the years, your inspiring work with the Almond Branch, and the beautiful work you did in editing and publishing this book.

Juliah Bornick What started off as a simple proof-read turned into an excellent grammatical upgrade — thank you so much for your investment in this project. I don't think it was a coincidence that you ended up helping with the copy editing on this book!

To those who took the time to review draft copies and provide me with feedback, I am deeply grateful — Binu Jacob, Steve Farrar, Dave and Kay Carringer, Katherine Lee, Bob Young, Leilani Rector, and Randy Bonser.

The Love-Breath That Whispered the Universe Into Existence Is Breathing Through You Now

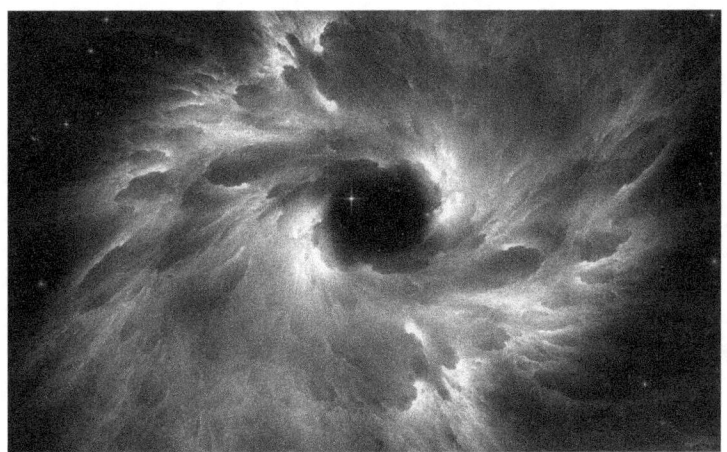

The Divine Community:

Throughout the book, you'll see the words "They" and "Them" when referring to the Divine. This is a reminder that "God" is a relational Being, existing eternally as a Community of Love into which we are included. God is also beyond gender, while embodying all the best masculine and feminine characteristics. For example, there are many mentions of the Divine Feminine in scripture, so I use "She" on occasion, referring to Holy Spirit or Lady Wisdom. I believe They are fond of me using these terms of affection and honor for Them!

Contents

Prologue	Invitation – Earthquake of the Soul	13
Part I	**A Garden in the Abyss**	**19**
Chapter 1	Initiation – The Abyss	21
Chapter 2	Illustration – Sanctuary of the Divine	35
Chapter 3	Interpretation – A Wholesale Remodeling Project	49
Chapter 4	Integration – Bookends of the Story	69
Chapter 5	Inspiration – Creation, the Original Scriptures	73
Chapter 6	Infestation – Something Sinister This Way Slithers	85
Chapter 7	Imitation – Rise of the Deepfake	93
PART II	**Awakening the True Self**	**105**
Chapter 8	Incarnation – Arrival of Our True Mirror	107
Chapter 9	Implication – Christ-Expression in the World	121
Chapter 10	Instigation — Quantum Physics and the Kingdom	129
Chapter 11	Impartation – The Omega-Point	157
Chapter 12	Imagination – A Final Fascination	165

Prologue

Invitation – Earthquake of the Soul

On the last weekend in January 2006, I gave up on my Christianity. At the time, I could never have imagined the bizarre path this decision would lead me toward...one that ended up dropping me inside a black hole and altering everything I thought I knew about reality.

Leaving the Faith

At some point along our journey, some of us who grew up in a religious tradition start questioning our long-held beliefs. Sometimes, these questions lead us down pathways that are unfamiliar to our minds and hearts. This is perfectly normal, and God LOVES our authentic questions. I'm not sure that true growth can take place without them.

At times, however, this process can be frustrating, frightening, and fiercely confrontational. Perhaps our questions are offensive to friends and family members who now see us as careless heretics because they perceive our doubts and questions to be dangerous. It might feel like we're losing our foundation and that all we've known has become uncertain. Our souls may experience the unbearable weight of loneliness as we go through the process of faith-deconstruction.

It was all this for me and more. At times, it was absolutely terrifying, and often I was unsure if I would emerge with anything left. No one around me really knew what was going on, not even my family. I kept it under wraps and continued with many of the same routines, while inside my soul, tectonic plates were shifting and breaking up the foundations of my belief systems. I simply couldn't ignore the possibility that I had completely missed it when it came to my understanding of God.

INTO THE ABYSS

From the time I was a kid, I was your basic Christian fundamentalist do-gooder who played by all the morality rules. Never drank, never smoked, swore, used drugs, or did anything that I thought God would hold against me in His heavenly court of law. I had read hundreds upon hundreds of books, listened to thousands of sermons, and memorized vast portions of Scriptures, which I thought were all God-sanctioned confirmations of my robust, accurate theology, anchored firmly in established doctrines of the church. I had spent most of my life passionately defending my beliefs against any and all differing perspectives. From this rather self-assured mindset, I only "received" things that reinforced my existing worldview, and cautious fear kept me from exploring anything outside of my carefully constructed theological mansion...until my mansion came crashing down.

Some major plate-shifts in and around me were threatening to rip apart my faith for quite some time—circumstances were spiraling out of my control, causing me to question many of the foundational beliefs I had been taught since childhood. Several primary sources of security on which I had built my entire life were being destroyed, and these shifts turned into a series of earthquakes that continued to climb up the Richter scale with each passing day.

I watched wide-eyed in horror as I lost my great engineering job of 19 years. We lost our house to a foreclosure, declared bankruptcy, and experienced devastation as our oldest child started experimenting with drugs. This, coupled with other conflicts at home, while seeing yet another marriage counselor, not to mention the weight of my parents' deep disappointment in what was happening, was almost more than I could bear. In all of this, I lost hope for my lifelong "successful Christian life" image, and soon I abandoned any sense of future vision.

All the wonderful, spiritual things that I had done for God apparently meant nothing to Him. This led me to believe He was ignoring His promises in scripture to faithful followers like me about the "good life" I was supposed to be enjoying. This series of unfortunate events was all in the background as the theological foundation that had kept me safe and well-insulated for many decades crumbled. To make it worse, my break from childhood tradition drew severe criticism from family and long-time friends (and still does). I was lost. Yes...God was letting me down; of that I was quite sure. And I didn't know whether He would ever pursue me again.

PROLOGUE: INVITATION – EARTHQUAKE OF THE SOUL

A Child's Simple Request

After a few difficult years attempting to navigate a doozy of a deconstruction mainly on my own, I approached the Divine and asked Them to teach me about Reality...as if I didn't already know what that meant. I think God enjoyed that audacious, childlike request! Lady Wisdom began unveiling various facets of beauty that were foreign to my thinking. She connected me with several faith communities (including some that were online) who were navigating very similar "crashes" in their journeys. This was a wonderful gift for my soul. Wisdom also showed me some amazing images in the realm of science as I studied the Creation—the original scripture. Exploring these images eventually drew me back to a sense of awe and wonder.

And faith.

However, most of my robust, painstakingly built "theological mansion" became completely demolished along the way. What arose in its place involved less certainty and more mystery, a letting go of my desperate need to have it all figured out, and an openness to discovering what lay ahead. There's so much I realized that I simply didn't know, and I had to set many of my "certainties" aside to continue this journey of discovery.

One thing I do know for certain and have become fully persuaded of is this - God is pure Love, and everything else we know about His character... *Their character*...aligns with Love. My internal portraits of God have become far more beautiful as a result, though I'm well aware that "God" exists light-years beyond my/our most eloquent concepts about Them.

It took me most of my life to realize that God isn't a bottled genie that promises to take away all of our pain and suffering, a cosmic magician conjuring a lavish life of smooth sailing the whole way home. I have struggled, and still do, with fear, doubt, depression, and apathy. Though I am sometimes too overwhelmed to think straight, this excruciating process finally brought me to the point where I felt the freedom to admit my pain and weakness, with no need to pretend that I had it all together.

Amid the joy and chaos, and sometimes unspeakable agony of everyday existence, I have tasted of an intoxicating Love I cannot escape or unsee. This Love has become my assurance and hope—a light that shines steadily amidst the shadows floating in and out of my inner being. It is with tender compassion that They suffer *with* me—and with all who bear Their image.

INTO THE ABYSS

Take heart, dear friend...God does NOT leave us to wander or suffer alone. Spirit is overjoyed with us as we embark on our journey, because She sees that it's leading us to discover our True Selves. Within the chaos lies the ultimate Beauty that our soul has been seeking. I've come to view this sometimes-painful process as a "burning away" of all that is not Christ, a simplifying down to the bare essentials, then "reconstructing" our perspectives on the foundation of God's beautiful character.

And what a true, tender and trustworthy Guide we've been given for this burning away; One Who comes to us as the All-Consuming Fire of Holy Love. The journey into the unknown is worth it, for in the darkness, God is waiting...arms wide open and eyes shining with anticipation.

> **Exodus 20:21 (NLT)** "...the people stood at a distance, but Moses approached the Thick Darkness, **where God was**."

Three Pillars

The ancients referred to three pillars upon which society rests: *Truth, Goodness, and Beauty*. For centuries, we have focused almost exclusively on defending Truth (apologetics) and demanding Goodness (ethics, morality) in our faith traditions, virtually to the downright dismissal of displaying Beauty (aesthetics). But Beauty alone, it seems, carries within itself a strange power able to transport us back to a state of childlike wonder. It provides a stealth entry to the deep recesses of the human heart, cleverly bypassing the natural defense systems that many of us have constructed over the years. And when our soul encounters true Beauty, it creates space for Truth and Goodness to flourish as well.

In my journey, I found this missing piece made all the difference. A sense of innocent awe and hopeful expectation belongs to those that can become like children, not just as an entry point for belief, but rather as a way of ongoing discovery rooted in the sacred mysteries. Our childlike hearts long to be swept into a vast, all-encompassing Story...an epic of such beauty that it steals our breath away. I desire to place before you a compelling, universe-sized portrait of the epic, eternal Christ Story into which we have all been included, and together discover how this beautiful Story brings us face to face with who we really are.

PROLOGUE: INVITATION – EARTHQUAKE OF THE SOUL

Soul Cravings

Seeking God
  Is exhilarating
    But dangerous.

They rarely show up
  To affirm that everything
    We are doing and believing
      Is completely correct.

Rather, They come to
  Challenge, Confront and
    Craft us into the people
      They know we already are.

It's done out of Love . . .
  But it's rarely safe
    And hardly ever predictable.

So . . .
Are you hoping
For safe, predictable, manageable?
What does your DEEPEST SOUL . . . truly crave?

Let go of what you think you
Know for certain, and
let God teach
You.

INTO THE ABYSS

I have included some "**REFLECTION**" opportunities throughout the book where I invite you to take an *11-second deep breath...to pause and exercise your imagination.

> *Note: I love number strings like 11:11:11, so taking an 11-second deep breath carries a childlike delight for me. That said, there's nothing inherently special about "11." When I practice meditation, I find a quiet place, get into a relaxed, comfortable position, and close my eyes. Then I slowly inhale for four seconds, hold for three, then exhale for four—*the four-three-four deep breath*. I repeat this several times until I connect to the deep part of my spirit that is joined to God, the invitation to "enter my center." While breathing, I like to hold a single thought or image in my mind and heart, giving it the freedom to expand within my imagination. Feel free to improvise!

Some of these ideas may take longer than 11 seconds to consider:

Pause, Breathe,
Reflect, Meditate, Marinate,
Noodle, Doodle, Contemplate, Visualize,
Paint, Play, Imagine, Dream, Walk, Wander, Return

Part I
A Garden in the Abyss

*Sometimes, astounding beauty is
hidden in the most unusual places.*

*"The first gulp from the glass of natural sciences
will turn you into an atheist, but
at the bottom of the glass
God is waiting
for you."*

Werner Heisenberg
German physicist, awarded Nobel Prize
for "the creation of quantum mechanics" in 1932

Chapter 1
Initiation – The Abyss
(Deep Space)

"We see the world...NOT as IT is...but as WE are."
Adapted from the Talmud[1]

Artist's rendering of a Black Hole at the center of the Milky Way galaxy[2]

At the heart of existence lies a throbbing, eternal, boundless flow of pure life. The essence of this flow is a shared, intimate love that pulses in and through the Source of all, the Reality that we call "God." We were conceived within this flow of love. This is our true home, our original birthplace.

---

1. Babylonian Talmud: Tractate Berakoth, Folio 55b, Boston: New Talmud Publishing Society, 1916.
2. National Geographic, April 11, 2017, https://news.nationalgeographic.com/content/dam/news/2017/04/11/black-hole/black-hole-event-horizon-01.ngsversion.1491940808945.adapt.1900.1.jpg.

INTO THE ABYSS

Approaching a Black Hole

It was the fall of 2012, and I was lying in bed late one night staring up at the ceiling, unable to sleep. We had recently declared bankruptcy on our way to losing our previous home to an illegal foreclosure, which had left me traumatized and feeling like an utter failure. I suffered from depression and showed signs of PTSD from the horrific memory of being evicted from our home in 24 hours, without having a single thing packed and ready. We were... HOMELESS?!? The shame in my soul was simply overwhelming, especially in our proud Indian culture where things like this simply weren't on the radar for hard-working, rule-following, Bible-memorizing middle-class families like ours. Maybe this trauma was the final interior earthquake in a decade-long series of quakes that left me with a deep and gaping void, crying out for relief.

Suddenly, the ceiling appeared to open, and I was jettisoned out of the bedroom and upwards into the atmosphere. In the next moment, I was being sucked toward a gigantic vortex in deep space at nearly the speed of light. Surrounding me was space junk of all shapes and sizes, as the chaotic fury of a near-infinite force pulled everything toward its center.

I became painfully aware of my fast-approaching fate, hurtling toward a deep, dark, cavernous void, frightened out of my mind. About to be swallowed whole by something that existed far beyond my wildest imagination, this was going to be the end of myself as I knew "me" to be. I knew that I was in something like a radical lucid vision, but the kind where you wake up with elements from the dream world deposited into the real one. Many moons later, I would come to understand that *I was experiencing a mystical journey into a supermassive black hole.*

From a very young age, science has intrigued me. In my 20s and 30s, I was fascinated by astronomy, and this later launched me into black holes and connected me with quantum physics. Even now, these delicious topics remain my true delight. Let me pause here and attempt to describe what black holes are. They are quite an example of how truth is stranger and far more bizarre than (science) fiction.

Black Holes: *Formation* [3]

Black holes form in space when stars or other massive objects collapse from their own gravity. For most of a star's lifetime, the force of radiation shooting outward (its light) is balanced with the force of gravity pulling

---

3. Oliver, Neal, *The Black hole: Astrophysics for People*, Amazon.com Services LLC, April 20, 2020.

CHAPTER 1: INITIATION – THE ABYSS

inward. This tension keeps the star in existence. As the star's nuclear fuel is exhausted, the outward forces of radiation diminish, allowing the massive force of gravity to compress the star inward. This contraction into the core causes its temperature to rise and allows its remaining materials to be used as fuel. Eventually, this nuclear fuel is expended, and the core collapses. If the star is sufficiently massive or compressible, it collapses into a black hole. The star essentially becomes a tiny dot with a density that is near infinite.

Event Horizon

Around the center of a black hole is a boundary called the event horizon, and once anything crosses this boundary, the gravity from the vortex is so strong that nothing can escape. Essentially, it is the point-of-no-return. Anything that passes the event horizon is heading into the center of the black hole. As soon as an object passes within this ferocious boundary, it is completely lost to the outside universe. Anything inside the event horizon cannot be retrieved to study. It belongs to the realm of the unknown.

Singularity

At the center of a black hole lies the singularity, where matter is crushed to infinite density.[4] The pull of gravity is infinitely strong here, and space-time has infinite curvature. Imagine a supermassive star, billions of times the mass of our sun (and keep in mind that over a million earths can fit into our one sun). Imagine that this unspeakably massive star is condensed down to a tiny piece of candy that you can place on your finger! This analogy will help you realize the phenomenon that scientists worldwide recognize as an astronomical marvel of unimaginable proportions. Jumbled up at this tiny singularity, *space and time cease to exist as we know them*. No one knows exactly what happens when something passes through the center of a black hole.

Entanglement and Quantum Field [5]

When it comes to singularities and unimaginably small things, there is something strange in the subatomic world that we should bring into our discussion. When two subatomic particles have merged, something fascinating happens after they are separated, even by a great distance. Scientists have found that when an action is performed on one particle, the other responds simultaneously. It's like the particles "know" they've once been part of each

---

4. Gott III, J.Richard, et al. "A Map of the Universe." The Astrophysical Journal, vol. 624, no. 2, IOP Publishing, May 2005, pp. 463–84.

5. Ziad Masri, *Reality Unveiled*, Awakened Media, 2017

other and want to stay joined together, even though now they are far apart. They are said to be "entangled." Einstein called this strange phenomenon "spooky action at a distance" because it calls our basic assumptions about reality into question.[6] Subatomic particles that have been "together" (like within a singularity) and are then split apart, remain energetically connected—even if they are on other ends of the universe! The entire universe is connected this way, in what scientists call the *quantum field* of energy.

OK. Let me summarize and save you from mind-tilt as your eyes begin to glaze over.

A massive star in the sky, sometimes millions or billions of times the mass of our sun, implodes upon itself and ends up becoming an infinitely small dot, able to fit (per se) on the tip of a needle. This collapsed state creates an enormous gravitational field from which nothing, not even light, can escape. Around this "dot" there's a spherical boundary called the *event horizon*. Once anything crosses that boundary, it immediately becomes invisible to the outside world. It's now headed into the center of the black hole, and nothing can stop it. We can fantasize about the details of what occurs inside a black hole, but we'd be mostly making stuff up. We are staring into a gaping abyss of unknown mystery, a mystery that intricately connects the entire universe.

Fearfully Fun Facts

- If you were to drop a small piece of candy into a black hole, the gravitational force is so strong it would generate the energy of an atomic bomb.
- If you were to detonate 1000 atomic bombs every second for over 13 billion years, you would still fall far short of the energy that's released in the final moments <u>when a single giant star</u> collapses into a black hole.
- The supermassive black hole at the center of the nearby Andromeda galaxy weighs about 100,000,000 times as much as the sun, or 333 trillion (that's trillion, with a *t*) times the weight of the earth.

Exploration of Reality

The world's most brilliant scientists have been exploring these phenomena over many decades, using cutting edge technology, utilizing our most advanced calculations and experimental findings from astrophysics, general relativity, string theory, and loop quantum gravity. Yet, they freely admit that we are

---

6. "The Nobel Prize in Physics 1921." *NobelPrize.org*, 10 May 2019, www.nobelprize.org/prizes/physics/1921/einstein/biographical/.

CHAPTER 1: INITIATION – THE ABYSS

confronted with an astounding mystery on the other side of the black hole. Even though research shows that most large galaxies, including our own Milky Way, contain at their center a black hole that is essentially responsible for shaping the entire galaxy around it, these universe-bending marvels have generated more questions than answers. And this is magnificent! It creates in the research community an intense desire to continue exploring, learning, discovering.

Both science and theology are, at their essence, motivated by the exploration of Reality. Any unbiased look at the Creation, either through a telescope or microscope, will eventually lead a person toward ultimate reality. And it's a beautiful thing when a focused gaze captures something spectacular at the heart of the entire universe.

> *"My experiences with science led me to God.*
> *They challenge science to prove the existence of God.*
> *But must we really light a candle to see the sun?"*
> **Wernher von Braun**[7]

Just as in the sacred written Scriptures, the Spirit of God leaves us clues in Her universe (the "scriptures" of Creation), which draw us toward Truth. At the end of any authentic scientific endeavor—one that sparks from true curiosity and is absent existing bias—are the fingerprints of the Creator, identifying and declaring the story of Creation. Abba speaks to us ever so creatively...if we could just learn to listen...to be still, and "know that I AM God" (see Ps. 46:1).

M87: The First Black Hole Photo Ever

On Wednesday, April 10, 2019, scientists produced the first image of a black hole in a "nearby" galaxy called Messier 87 (M87 for short, located about 55 million light-years away).[8] It wasn't an image of the black hole itself, but essentially the shadow or silhouette of the hole against the surrounding glow of the event horizon, that boundary beyond which nothing, not even light, can escape. It is wider than our entire solar system, and its mass is calculated to be about 6.5 billion (with a *b*) times the mass of our sun. This work is heralded as among the greatest astronomical breakthroughs of this past century.

---

7. Von Braun, Werner. Letter to the California State board of Education (14 September 1972)

8. Landau, Elizabeth. "Black Hole Image Makes History" May 8, 2019. Accessed Feb 13, 2020. https://www.nasa.gov/mission_pages/chandra/news/black-hole-image-makes-history

INTO THE ABYSS

You may be familiar with the classic image of a message in a bottle. Someone on an island far away slips a critical message into a glass bottle and sets it out to sea. They hope that the message would make its way across the far reaches of the ocean into someone else's hands. In the same way, God has put messages into different vessels of creation for us to uncork and "read." Some of these messages travel across oceans of starlight and unfathomable stretches of time in hopes of reaching our eyes. This recent photograph of M87's black hole is one such vessel that has just recently hit the shoreline of our telescopes.

An important note...The name given to this black hole was "Powehi," which comes from the Kumulipo, an 18th-century Hawaiian creation chant, and carries the meaning "adorned fathomless dark source of unending creation." I love this name!

After reflecting for some time on these cosmic wonders of our galaxies, and specifically this M87 photo, a handful of thoughts came to mind. These five points lay some important groundwork for the journey ahead, including the context for the experience that I'll share in the next chapter.

1. Mystery: The Awe-Inspiring Nature of Reality

Inside the center of a black hole is...great mystery. This recent photographic breakthrough confirms that we are just scratching the surface of what we know about our universe. We are like toddlers staring at complex calculus on a colossal canvas, recognizing hints of a few letters, shapes, and colors, pretending we understand all that we're seeing.

In the same way, our exploration of God is still in its infancy. We are only a few thousand years into our study of the Divine; however, we believe we have already come to see and experience all that's necessary about Reality. It reminds me of the passage toward the end of the book of Job, where God thunders forth a speech about the creation narrative so magnificently that it leaves Job reeling in stunned, repentant silence.

When we operate from confident religious certainty in these times that require us to explore with a sense of mystery and wonder, we are effectively silencing our voice in society. Black holes invite us back to a place of childlike curiosity and awe, desperately calling out for us to infuse those qualities into our theology. God is not the "unknowable" or the "already known." Rather, They are *endlessly knowable*. We have simply been given the gift of eternal discovery, which is meant to begin now and last forever. Our joyful

CHAPTER 1: INITIATION – THE ABYSS

privilege is to share Christ's beauty with the wide eyes of a child uncovering a world full of delights, enough for everyone—not laying out a certain set of strict boundaries and beliefs to get on the good side of God's favor.

After all, the people Jesus threatened severely while here on earth were those that thought they had arrived at the whole truth through their diligent study and detailed knowledge of their sacred Scriptures. Attitudes of certainty and exclusivity brought down His scathing criticism, as the credentialed religious elite quickly realized, to their horror and shame. I eventually realized that this was precisely the approach I had taken, to my utter horror and shame. As a believer in God, my main goal was to defend the staunch certainty I had about my exclusive belief system.

With that as a backdrop, these days, I am certain about a whole lot less than I used to be and am convinced that my experience of God will continue to require several significant shifts as the journey continues. The thing is, I'm no longer aiming for certainty; I'm aiming to learn the art of trust and the rhythms of Grace, with the childlike humility to admit my need for growth in so many areas of my life. I want to be fully open to what is placed before me.

We will all find one day that we were **gloriously wrong** in so many areas, including key aspects of our doctrines and beliefs. Christ, and the Story into which we've been included, will exceed our greatest imagination in every way possible. God's love, holiness, mercy, justice, grace, wrath, and wisdom will surpass our most eloquent descriptions and drop our collective jaws to the earth.

I hope we can agree on this.

2. Community: Unified Vision

Man has been studying the skies since the dawn of time, especially since 1608 when the first telescope was invented. As our tools have steadily advanced, we've been able to see more and more detail, and the mystery keeps increasing. Recent leaps in technology, like the ABYSS Ultra Deep Field images from the Hubble Telescope, have allowed us to "see" further into ancient history, as light from galaxies that *started its journey 13.2 billion years ago* is just now reaching our field of view. Looking at that same slice of sky in 1700 may have yielded a clear view of a few distant stars. But as our awareness grew and our technology advanced—and especially as cooperation among scientists improved—so did the number (and details) of heavenly bodies that came into view.

INTO THE ABYSS

As one example, the EHT (Event Horizon Telescope) project is a consortium of over 200 scientists working together for over 20 years. It affectionately takes its name from that famous boundary point of no return. There was no single telescope on earth capable of making the necessary observation of M87's black hole, so the team had to get creative. The researchers linked up radio telescopes in Arizona, Mexico, Antarctica, Spain, and 11 other locations worldwide to form a virtual instrument the size of the entire earth.

"Doing physics is a dialog with nature," one of the researchers reportedly said in describing the process of collecting and analyzing the massive amounts of data necessary to generate these images. What a conversation this has been and will continue to be! The scientists working on this project believe that these discoveries could change the way we perceive ourselves as humans and our place in the cosmos.

While the EHT towers were collecting data, another instrument in space—the Chandra X-ray observatory—was focused on this same black hole's home galaxy for the past 20 years. As it orbited the earth, four ultrasensitive mirrors on Chandra captured the X-ray radiation of multi-million-degree gas shrouding M87, coming from the high-energy particles that the black hole was flinging into space. This allowed Chandra to take a "wide-angle" shot of the same black hole and all that surrounds it.

Sometimes, it's good to stand from a distance and consider a "wide-angle" shot of our faith traditions beyond the boundaries of the traditions themselves. Our sacred text tells us that we have the mind of Christ, and yet we count over 41,000 different denominations within Christianity alone! Wait, what?!?

Part of the issue here is that influential leaders in particular streams have created great animosity and conflict by fiercely alienating themselves from other traditions, and in some cases, condemning them outright. This is all because they often perceive themselves to be the sole arbiters of correct scriptural interpretation. The large number of denominations isn't the issue. That's only a symptom of something much deadlier underneath—a religious mindset that relies on certainty and exclusion, rather than the unity that comes from an intense focus on the central, unifying Reality of Christ.

God is inviting us to envision a "global lens" through which we can see the beauty of Christ. Over the course of history, we've seen what has happened as people received insights and revelations about God and then started huddling around those revelations. Instead of 41,000 splintered factions meeting to desperately protect their individual findings, what if we freely shared them

CHAPTER 1: INITIATION – THE ABYSS

with others—not to prove who was right about our limited insights and interpretations, but to continue discovering what was beautiful and compelling and true about Christ? This type of diversity and creative differences give us reason for celebration, unlike the clearly marked lines of separation that characterize our existing structures today.

Scientists across the globe created an "earth-sized telescope" with which to see this black hole. No one single telescope could have done this on its own. Instead, they merged the views from ALL of the individual lenses, integrated the information gathered over 20 years, then joyfully displayed something magnificent. Any sense of competition, barriers, or pride regarding individual discoveries gave way to their shared desire to see what was far greater than any one source could see alone. When each EHT site saw its role as contributing to a larger vision, the scope of possibility expanded dramatically.

Black holes are drawing us toward a much larger shared vision of what's possible when "we" join together in contemplating and then expressing the Christ. We find a glimpse of this God-sized vision in John 17, where Jesus speaks to the Father about His disciples:

> **John 17:17-23 (VOICE)** Immerse them in the truth, the truth Your voice speaks. In the same way You sent Me into this world, I am sending them. It is entirely for their benefit that I have set Myself apart so that they may be set apart by truth. I am not asking solely for their benefit; this prayer is also for all the believers who will follow them and hear them speak. Father, may they all be one as You are in Me and I am in You; may they be in Us, for by this unity the world will believe that You sent Me.
>
> All the glory You have given to Me, I pass on to them. May that glory unify them and make them one as We are one, I in them and You in Me, that they may be refined so that all will know that You sent Me, and You love them in the same way You love Me.

This larger shared vision has already begun to spread across the globe.

3. Singularity: Christ, the Container of the Cosmos

Remember, a black hole is the collapse of a massive star into a tiny, tiny point that is invisible, even under an electron microscope. Imagine that instead of just a single star, the *entire universe* is condensed into a point like this. This is exactly what happened at the beginning of time—the moment the universe was created—where all that exists was contained in one Singularity. Scientists call this the origin of the universe—the "First Cause." Our scriptures call this *Christ*.

Christ is the Singularity in which the entire cosmos exists.

Paul, in his letter to the Colossians, describes this entire-universe-in-Christ-ness as follows:

> **Col. 1:15-16 (AMPC)** For it was *in Christ* that all things were created, in heaven and on earth, things seen and things unseen, whether thrones, dominions, rulers, or authorities; all things were created and exist through Him [by His service, intervention] and *in and for Him*.
>
> And He Himself existed before all things, and *in Him all things consist* (cohere, are held together).

We see here that our starting point as we frame our theology is our connection to Christ—not our connection to sin. In Genesis 1:1, we see this overarching theme of the Creation narrative. In the beginning, God created the heavens and the earth. But this isn't a God who creates, surveys Their handiwork, and then heads off to a distant heaven to take care of other pressing matters in the universe. The whole of Creation was created in Christ. All that exists—time, space, matter, energy, and consciousness—was created in Him and is now sustained and held together in Him, even at this very moment. God's essence is present in every aspect of the cosmos, down to each subatomic particle.

This evidence demolishes any possible notion of separation between God and man. How can we be separated from the Source and Sustenance of our very existence...of *all* existence...of the breath that gives life? It's impossible. Yes, man *believed* he was separated from God, but this wasn't actually true. We only "thought" we were. It may be convincing because we've heard it for so long, so often, from so many different people. Thankfully, we are slowly waking up to the reality of our true origin. Science is helping affirm our need to start the story at the very beginning with a Singularity. Our beginning point is Genesis 1, where all things are intimately connected (in Christ)—not Genesis 3, where we started seeing God and ourselves through fallen and distorted lenses.

CHAPTER 1: INITIATION – THE ABYSS

This vantage point also demolishes any possible notion of our separation from anything in the Creation, including each other. We are entangled at the subatomic level with everything that exists because we participate in the quantum field.[9] All things are "energetically connected" to each other because of their common ancestry within the Singularity. As we'll see later, this has some amazing implications.

These premises about our shared origin are foundational to the Gospel. The universe, and everything in it, was created, sustained, and (will forever be) held together **in Christ** (see Colossians 1). God is the One in whom we live, move, and have our being (see Acts 17) and the One Who fills everything everywhere with Themselves (see Ephesians 1-4). We are in a mysterious, glorious union with the Source of all, and with all that exists...branches on the Vine, the One in Whom we enjoy our very existence. Astrophysicists call this phenomenon the "Singularity" of the universe and the resulting "field" that connects the entire Creation. Though they aren't using religious language when describing their findings, modern scientists highlight the same universe-beginning and cosmos-sustaining Reality that our Scriptures describe as God.

4. Possibility: A Blank Whiteboard

Before the Creation event, before space and time, everything existed as pure possibility. Our entire universe was contained in an infinitely dense dot, ready to explode into existence. The intricate orchestration and precision required for this Singularity to eventually become what we now know as the Cosmos *is all contained within Christ*.

Before Creation began, I imagine God knowing every single possibility of every single thing that could ever take place throughout the universe's existence—every activity and interaction in every cubic millimeter of space and every nanosecond of time—*already* having responses in place *as if* each of those possibilities were a certainty. In other words, in the beginning, the future was filled with the freedom of wide-open possibilities, not scripted, pre-determined, or blueprinted ahead of time.

Let's use a chess analogy. If God were playing a game of chess, They would know every one of the nearly infinite possible combinations of moves, and plan responses to every one of them ahead of time so that ultimately They gain victory in the end. God doesn't predetermine the universe's actions, but rather anticipates these moves and responds in wisdom and creativity in

---

9. Lancaster, T., & Blundell, S. (2014). Quantum field theory for the gifted amateur.

line with Their nature of love. The Story is not a prescribed blueprint being robotically played out, but an interconnected collection of nearly infinite possibilities, with a planned response to each of them.

If it's true that God knows ALL things—some of these things being certainties and other things being possibilities—then existence is a blank whiteboard, and we are free to participate in the beautiful, organic Story of God unfolding before us. We can be fully persuaded that God has already planned options in place for every combination/permutation of possibilities throughout all of time and space, including every detail of our earthly lives.

The victory of Love is certain...Love endures all things and will not fail. The end game is a given, and *Love will have the final word*. Yet possibilities along the way to that place of victory are nearly endless. And these possibilities are all connected because of their entanglement in the Singularity.

This framework of how the future unfolds seems to reconcile the authenticity of God's emotions (sadness, joy, anger, surprise) without the need to "pretend"...as would seemingly be the case if all things were known as certainties ahead of time.

It also allows for Their genuine participation with us as we experience daily existence, and highlights Their confidence to entrust certain aspects of the future (possibilities) to humanity because of outcomes that God alone knows and plans (certainties). And all of this future possibility was and is housed within the Christ-Singularity. The chess analogy falls apart when we realize the chessboard, the pieces, the participants, and the environment in which it's being played are all contained *in Christ*. We're attempting to define infinite wisdom with limited human examples.

Bottom Line: This God of infinite creativity and wisdom can be trusted in all things, at all times, with our whole lives. Christ is our Certainty amidst the near-infinite possibilities that life brings, and this assurance brings enormous freedom to our souls.

5. Identity: Who We Are

The last item, identity, will take us into the next chapter where we'll dive into the rest of my black hole experience. As we head there, I'll warn you that the scenes I witnessed didn't fall into any mental categories that

CHAPTER 1: INITIATION – THE ABYSS

I had at the time, so I apologize if my descriptions don't quite capture all that I experienced. I believe that the essence of God's Creation-birthing and Universe-sustaining Love weaves its way through.

The diagram below will be beneficial as we move forward. It helps to visualize the made-in-God's-image framework that describes how mankind is comprised of a spirit, soul, and body.[10] It's a simple model that allows us to portray the part of us that is aware of God (spirit), aware of self (soul), and aware of the world around us (body). This framework provides us with a common language to describe the inner dynamics of the way humans interact with and relate to God, ourselves, and each other. We'll need this diagram as a reference for when we approach the black hole.

IDENTITY MODEL: SPIRIT, SOUL, AND BODY

I had always assumed that maturity in my spiritual journey was mainly about steady forward movement, but as it turns out, God first wanted me to go backward—way, way back—to the origin of our universe. So...I'd like to invite you with me to the very beginning, and use it as a gateway through which we might encounter the ultimate Reality that we call God.

---

10. Watchman Nee, *Spiritual Man*, Christian Fellowship Publishers, Inc; Reprint edition, 1968.

Chapter 2

Illustration – Sanctuary of the Divine
(pre-Genesis)

> *"Heaven is the Song*
> *We were all born*
> *Remembering."*
>
> **Anonymous**

There's a roller coaster called the Top Thrill Dragster at Cedar Point amusement park in Sandusky, Ohio, where riders are launched horizontally from 0 to 120 miles per hour in less than four seconds.[11] It's like being shot out of a cannon! It is a crazy insane-in-the-membrane adrenaline rush, loved by thrill fans across the globe, including me. Now imagine racing toward an abyss at *186,000 miles per second* (you heard correctly).

I was heading into the dead center of a black hole.

Backward in Time

Recall from the first chapter that I was being sucked toward a gigantic vortex, surrounded by an "event horizon," at nearly the speed of light. The center of this vortex, the dimensionless "dot" supplying it with its monstrous gravitational pull, was the beginning point of space and time, the birth of the universe as we know it today. It's the moment that the author of Genesis describes as "in the beginning," and it was billions of light-years away from where I had just been lying in bed, staring up at the ceiling.

---
11. Cedar Point amusement park. Sandusky, OH. https://www.cedarpoint.com/play/rides/top-thrill-dragster

INTO THE ABYSS

Have you ever had a dream where you knew things without understanding how or why? It was like that in this experience. As I was thrown backward in time and space at a dizzying pace toward this beginning moment, I caught a series of strobe-like glimpses of my entire life and the entire span of human history surrounding my existence. Somehow, my conscious mind was able to grasp and process with strange clarity how all of it had influenced my present life and perspectives. I saw that "I" was essentially a compilation of *all the inputs that had come before*, molding and shaping me into the man I believed was me.

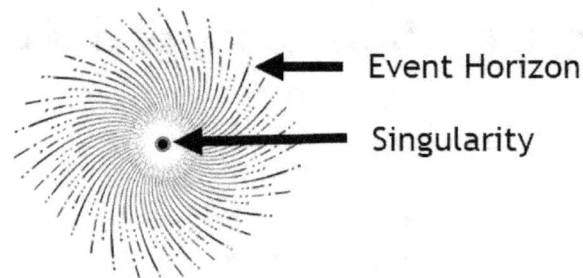

Image of Event Horizon and Black Hole Center

As these lightning-fast images were flashing before me, they suddenly stopped, and I found myself at the edge of the event horizon that surrounds the beginning of time, the moment of First Creation. There was an eerie silence as I skittered toward the boundary and skid to a screeching stop.

In that brief instant, my mind flashed back to the story of Creation I had learned in Genesis, the brilliant Jewish narrative describing the formation of the cosmos. In the beginning, God created...

A few deep questions crossed my mind in that same instant.

What was on the *other side* of that initial Creation moment?

What was going on *before* God began creating?

In the Beginning, God

The opening statement in the book of Beginnings brings to us an enormous declaration. As with all epic stories, the first scenes introduce the main characters, context, and perhaps the central themes that will later unfold. In the first four words, we see a distinct beginning to this

CHAPTER 2: ILLUSTRATION – SANCTUARY OF THE DIVINE

Story above all other stories, and most importantly, we meet the central character: God, the Uncreated One. In the Hebrew, this word for "God" is *Elohim* (אֱלֹהִים).

> **Gen. 1:1 (AMPC)** <u>In the beginning, God</u> created the heavens and the earth.
>
> **Gen. 1:26 (AMPC)** God said, "Let <u>Us</u> [Father, Son, and Holy Spirit] make mankind in <u>Our</u> image, after <u>Our</u> likeness . . ."

In light of these verses, there are two important things to be aware of—two "hints" about the Reality in Whom we exist:

> **Hint 1:** *Elohim* carries with it a **plural** connotation in the original Hebrew language.
>
> **Hint 2:** God speaks within an <u>Already Existing Community</u> before the Creation of man.

Black Hole Trip, continued...

OK, back to my cosmic ride toward the beginning of time, where the *entire universe* was condensed down to a single point. I had paused for a brief moment, just before crossing the boundary surrounding this point, but once I lifted the brakes, there was no turning back!

The moment I crossed the event horizon, I immediately hit light speed—186,000 miles per second—as I launched headfirst toward the center. In that very instant, I started to experience a beyond-science-fiction phenomenon called *spaghettification* as I rocketed toward the middle of the black hole, surrounded by space junk heading toward the same destination.[12]

Spaghettifi-what?

What in Jupiter's name is spaghettification?! Well, imagine a pasta machine, grinding and stretching, squeezing and slicing clumps of fresh pasta into long, thin strips of spaghetti. That gives a little idea of what black hole *spaghettification* is. Just like with pasta, this is what happens to anything that heads into a black hole's center. As I rushed toward the

---

12. World of Phenomena; Phenomena.org, accessed Feb 3, 2020. https://www.phenomena.org/space/spaghettification/

INTO THE ABYSS

Singularity, the massive tidal forces acting on me approached infinity, and my body started being stretched and stretched beyond recognition. The pain was absolutely excruciating as I rocketed through this cosmic pasta machine!

I was soon ripped apart limb from limb (quite literally) until I had separated into a million pieces, my entire body now just a random collection of molecular dust. Eventually, even my atoms and subatomic particles were torn away from each other until not a single aspect of my physical self remained. The debris around me was obliterated in the same way as the forces stretched and separated them into nothingness.

I was still aware of "myself" as I neared the center of Creation's black hole, fully aware of the deep, dark abyss about to swallow me whole—the realm that science recognizes as pure mystery. I was pure spirit, encased in the invisible shell of an innocent, newborn-like soul, no longer attached to any part of my physical body.

Bam!! "I" hit the Singularity and was assaulted with the overwhelming sensation of my invisible "soul;" that is, my sense of self-consciousness—my mind, will, and emotions. Or, in other words, my personality. This was being peeled away from my spirit. The spaghettification of my physical body at the event horizon had left me as soul and spirit, and now this phase left me without a distinct "soul" as it too vanished into nothingness.

Only my spirit remained.

My body and soul, functioning as a type of "avatar" projection for my spirit, were no longer present. All pain completely vanished as I plummeted through the center and tumbled into another realm.

Through the Wormhole

Slowly, I became aware of the pre-Creation Reality into which I had been so forcefully propelled. My body and soul could not survive this transition into the center. Only pure spirit, a sense of all-in-all Divine Consciousness (what the apostle Paul called the mind of Christ), existed on the other side of this Singularity. My 186,000 miles-per-second trip through the center, through the wormhole, was over. And I came to a complete rest.

The nature of my surroundings was surreal...no sense of time, or space, or physical matter. Just an overwhelming awareness of an eternal, uncontainable Presence. A pure Divine Flow pulsing with beautiful, intimately raw, and life-giving love beyond anything I had ever known. I was fully and completely present here and was aware of the Divine as fully and completely present to me.

CHAPTER 2: ILLUSTRATION – SANCTUARY OF THE DIVINE

Surrounding me was a breathtaking array of wild and vivid color waves, colors I had never encountered before, completely otherworldly and transcendent, penetrating my essence. I could not only "see" these waves; I could "hear," "smell," "feel," and "taste" them as well. My spirit was overwhelmed with the resonance I was experiencing. I was struck with a sense that I couldn't determine. It was either complete and utter emptiness or overflowing fullness... or maybe both at once? It was like being inside the pregnant womb of the entire cosmos, and it left me in hushed silence.

I knew this Flow was that which caused all things to come into existence—the Ground of all being, the Source of all Creation. I was immersed in *God, in Reality itself*. Our church language describing the Trinity—Father, Son, and Holy Spirit—is only our limited attempt to capture this uncreated Holy Relational Flow. This is what ancient church fathers and mothers called the "perichoresis," a Greek term that essentially means a "circle dance." It is a Reality that exists infinitely beyond words and language.

I was in the midst of the Divine Community before the Creation.

In this realm, I felt a reverent sense of "holiness," but not in any way like the concept of holiness I had inherited through my religious upbringing and training. This holiness was marked by a deep, abiding, other-worldly, set-apart, eternally beautiful, relational intimacy, shared freely and fully within this Sacred Sanctuary. And I was most certainly not alone here! This sense of deep intimacy was being shared by a vast multitude of interconnected human spirits participating in this holy flow—a mysterious unity, all of us sharing joyfully in the Life of God. None of the spirits were aware of themselves as separate beings, only as unique expressions of the Whole—like branches on a Vine, or waves on an Ocean. There was no sense of past or future, only the present. I had no beginning or end...I was inside an eternal "now" moment.

> **John 14:20 (NLT)** At that time, you will know that I am in the Father, you are in Me, and I am in you.

Billions upon billions of other spirits were sharing this space, participants in the flow of waves in this Ocean, each marked by a unique "kaleidoscopic color signature" that designated their identity. These spirit-beings were made of light, mostly transparent; each one appeared as a holographic image, with just enough definition to distinguish one from another. Each one was a fascinating fractal-like combination of some 100 trillion trillion colors spanning the entire frequency spectrum, stretching far beyond the normal visible light band available on earth. The specific mix of colors was wholly unique to each spirit-being, and frequencies from across the entire spectrum were represented. The ever-changing beauty of each color-infused being was stunning, overwhelming, perfect.

No words were spoken, but the communication was deep, relaxed, and intimate. Perhaps life-giving communion was a better way to describe it. We were communing fluently and effortlessly with each other. Silence was the language of choice, as thoughts and emotions were carried via wordless frequencies that needed no accompanying sound. Here, we knew and were known, without distortion, bias, or suspicion. This communion was altogether pure, authentic, holy.

As I rested in the awareness of my existence as a light-spirit-being, I realized that *nothing* from my history was present within me. There was no "personal memory" of any of the events or circumstances that had shaped my life, though I was perfectly aware that all of them existed on the other side of the Singularity—all the information was seemingly frozen in time at the event horizon, yet fully available for my access. These memories and events, and my thoughts and feelings about them, were definitely all "mine," but they were certainly not "me." Here, my connection with/in the Divine was now the only shaping event defining my identity. This was such a strange sensation as I had spent my entire life being defined by everything except this. I would need to give myself permission to let this sink in.

Before Creation, this eternally-in-love community in union was . . .The only Reality, and my only Identity.

Garden of Delights

Soon, I began to sense that these light-spirit-beings were being sustained in an impossibly large garden, vibrant with color and sound, smells and sensations and tastes, nourished by the holy flow of Love-Light pulsing within the Divine Community. As I navigated this space—more like an entire ecosystem—it was clear that this Garden WAS God, the environment in which

CHAPTER 2: ILLUSTRATION – SANCTUARY OF THE DIVINE

all these beings found their existence. This Garden of Delights (*G.o.D.* became my affectionate name for this pre-Creation realm) housed this vast collection of spirit-seeds, each one containing a unique extension of the Divine.

I saw that these beings were God-breathed spirits, beautiful expressions of God's very breath. Ahhhh! Each was a color-infused *breath-print* of God! I knew then that this breath-print would one day be deposited into an embryo at conception and would be a God-breathed expression of Their life, providing all that was needed to grow and develop as a human being.

Yes, this vast holographic Garden of Delights full of spirit-seeds was the Divine "soil" in which every human would come into existence. These same connected spirits, appearing to me as *outside* of time, would one day inhabit physical bodies *inside* of time and grow to become aware of themselves as human souls, filled with the Spirit-breath of life.

At this point, I was doing everything possible to soak in this ecstatic beauty beyond all beauty. I was aware this wild mystery drizzled with wonder hovered beyond my ability to comprehend, let alone describe in words. I know I've still missed many of the intricate details because I was overwhelmed with awe.

In human terms—but multiplied by 11 billion—here is an extremely limited and inadequate, but hopefully helpful, analogy to describe the relational "flow" that I saw happening within God—*Elohim*. Imagine the intimacy shared within a group of three life-long friends since childhood, getting together for a week-long vacation at their favorite Hawaiian beach resort, with their favorite foods, memories, activities, and dreams all framed by the beauty of intimate friendship. No masks, nothing to hide, absent of any fear. Absolutely enjoying the time of their lives, living in their "sweet spot," nothing hindering the closeness of their relationship with each other.

Can we imagine? The beautiful flow between Father, Son, and Spirit in unrestrained, holy party mode, delighting in each other within Their paradise of existence. Laughter and joy and purpose-filled celebration fill the space. Eternal and complete, lacking absolutely nothing, Their true essence on full display.

Imagine the three friends pausing to pull up another chair, then asking me to come to join them at the table. Instead of awkward silence because I didn't fit in, somehow, Their enthusiasm drew me in as a full-fledged participant in this party *as if* I had known Them all of my life, as if They had participated in every treasured memory and experience I had ever known. Mmmmm...Yes, this was the joy I was feeling here (times 11 billion).

Crucifixion in the Garden

As my spirit surfed across wild waves of color beyond description, all my senses were at peak engagement, and I sensed an intense white light at the center of this realm. Though this light was too bright to make out many details, I was aware of a scene before me that triggered familiar memories from my childhood. I saw the faint outline of a cross contrasted against the light.

An impression rose within my awareness of a man being beaten by soldiers. His flesh was ripped away in shards under the repeated battering of cruel cords lined with bits of stone and glass. Later, he would be nailed to the cross set before my vision.

Somehow, this man perfectly embodied the beauty of the Divine Flow surrounding me in this place. This was the crucified Jesus, the Representative of this pre-Creation realm that came to us in time and space as the full expression of God. At this moment, it became clear to me that the hints and shadows of this famous event—the crucifixion of Jesus—were actually present *prior* to Creation itself. Here are two scriptures that point to this stunning reality:

> **I Pet. 1:20 (NLT)** God chose him as your ransom long before the world began, but he has now revealed him to you in these last days.

> **Rev. 13:8 (AMPC)** ...the Lamb that was slain [in sacrifice] from the foundation of the world.

Here's what I knew at that moment without hesitation. This crucifixion act was a picture of the exact same spaghettification process that I had experienced when I was hurtling into Creation's first black hole. The tearing away of all but spirit, the deep place of connection to the Divine, was displayed here in the pre-Creation realm.

In other words, I realized I was being given a startling visual of my own co-crucifixion with Christ—what I'll call my *co-spaghettification*. Certain passages in scripture explain this mystery, such as Romans 6, Galatians

CHAPTER 2: ILLUSTRATION – SANCTUARY OF THE DIVINE

2, Ephesians 2, and Colossians 2. It is our union with Christ in His death, where all the influences from our soul and body were torn away, so the true essence of God could be revealed.

In this realm of beginning-before-the-beginning, I was catching a glimpse of the Lamb of God slain before the foundation of the world. As I focused on the scene before me, the illuminated cross, doused in bright white light, started coming into sharper focus. I had the strange but confident sense that this was the revelation of a Love above all Loves... overpowering and all-encompassing—God's essence.

My awareness began to flash to Jesus' Passion Week. To any bystander watching, this was just the gruesome death of a "common criminal." But disguised underneath the seemingly obvious ugliness of the events taking place that day was the true revelation of God. When the sky grew dark, and the temple curtains ripped asunder, the universe witnessed an Eternal Love that had always included us within the Divine Sanctuary. That first-century event was being foreshadowed here in pre-Creation.

Funeral Celebration: Truth Moves in Mysterious Ways

To participate in this Truth, **we must be spectators at our own funeral**. This experience must be visceral, raw, and real for it to carry a transformational impact on our hearts. I lived with the intellectual understanding of these things that I read in the scriptures for most of my life. But I never felt the intensity of what this meant in my personal life and circumstances until I felt the pain of my own crucifixion.

This truth-infused freedom resident in the cross is fully activated by way of *our own* horrific and glorious death. Our own spaghettification. The story shadowed in the pre-beginning crucifixion scene...shock of all shocks...featured me and you and all of humanity. This pre-Creation image of torture and death contained a permanently present portrait of you and me and all of humanity within Christ.

And our own personal transformation comes from experiencing the reality—that Christ died **as us**...

2 Cor. 5:14-15 (NLT) Christ loves compels us, because we are convinced that **one died for all, and therefore all died**. And He died for all, so that all those who live might live no longer to and for themselves, but to and for Him Who died and was raised again for their sake.

Heb. 2:9 (NASB) We see Jesus...because of the suffering of death, so that **by the grace of God he might taste death for everyone.**

What do I mean, my own death? Well, this isn't a mind game. "I" died with Christ; specifically the part of me that seeks its identity and purpose from anything external to my spirit. Crucifixion demonstrated the same process as black-hole-spaghettification—the painful but necessary stripping away of all but the raw essence of the Christ-spirit as my sole identity—an identity that is eternal and unchanging.

It turns out my "funeral" took place when Jesus died and included me in His death. My obituary is recorded in several places in scripture, particularly the passages I already mentioned. Yours is in there as well. Yet to simply stand as a reverent but distant observer before this death, drains it of its transforming power in our own lives.

The cross has been taught mainly as a cause for solemn celebration, a symbol of our need to worship Jesus and our belief that we owe Him an impossible debt because of what He did for us. Though there may be a hint of redeemable merit in this idea, it's our *participation* in this reality that supplies the power to live out the Christ-life.

It's when we come into the deep experience of our *co-spaghettification* with Christ that all lesser, temporary influences are stripped away, and we are drawn into transformative encounter with the eternal, true part of our nature. In essence, what's true of God is gloriously ours in full, by the wonder of Their gracious union with us. I was:

Crucified—Christ died with me, as me, to strip away my false self.

Buried—False external realities were placed in a permanent grave.

Raised—I was lifted into the awareness of my union with the Divine.

CHAPTER 2: ILLUSTRATION – SANCTUARY OF THE DIVINE

> ***Seated in Heavenly Places***—Confidence that Christ is existence itself.

In my essence, I discovered that just as with Jesus, there is more that defines my existence than just my exterior human body and my human personality. The apostle Paul asks us to see Jesus, and each other, after the spirit and not after the flesh. Our spirit is where our True Self resides, and this requires us to experience the Spirit of Christ as our reference point to enter fully into our *un-becoming*. We'll get to that in Part II.

> **2 Cor. 5:16 (AMPC)** Consequently, from now on we estimate and regard no one from a [purely] human point of view [in terms of natural standards of value]. [No] even though we once did estimate Christ from a human viewpoint and as a man, yet now [we have such knowledge of Him that] we know Him no longer [in terms of the flesh].

Reference Point

Our co-spaghettification with Christ reveals that the crucified Jesus is the most precise expression we have in the Scriptures of God's essence. It is other-centered, self-sacrificial, *agapē* Love, shared within the Divine Sanctuary from all eternity. Jesus willingly offered His life to show us the extent of God's Love for the entire world. This eternal Love is the central theme of God's nature, out of which all Their other character traits flow. When we get to Their core essence, we discover that God is Love—the very same Love that defines our core essence and animates our existence.

> **Heb. 1:2-3 (AMPC)** [But] in the last of these days He has spoken to us in [the person of a] Son, Whom He appointed Heir and lawful Owner of all things, also by and through Whom He created the worlds and the reaches of space and the ages of time [He made, produced, built, operated, and arranged them in order]. He is the sole expression of the glory of God [the Light-being, the out-raying or radiance of the Divine], and He is the perfect imprint and very image of [God's] nature, upholding and maintaining and guiding and propelling the universe by His mighty word of power...

If Jesus is the "sole expression of the glory of God, the radiance of the Divine," then the crucifixion is where the curtain is thrown back so that we can clearly see the horrific escalating pattern of human violence, exposing the evil "systems" that lead to this kind of scapegoating and bloody sacrifice. As we look deeper, we witness the majestic display of God's magnificent self-sacrificial love for the whole world, the "cure" for dismantling these evil systems. It is also the clearest display of God's mercy, justice, holiness, wrath, and grace.

It helps to picture the scriptures as a landscape, in which case the Gospels are like a mountain range, and the Passion of Jesus is the highest peak in that range. It is where we see the clearest, most magnificent revelation of God's character.

As with white light through a prism, the pure, unfiltered light of God's essential nature finds expression in all of the myriad colors that comprise Their beautiful essence, all of which are wholly integrated and in perfect harmony with their Source. Ahhh! This is what I was encountering here! The wild spectrum of polychromatic splendor, comprised of those 100 trillion trillion hues in this Garden of Delights, was displaying the stunning facets of God's awe-inspiring character.

Their love's pure white light illuminated the cross, acting as a triangular prism (perhaps a Trinitarian hint), and burst into these breathtaking, extraordinary colors. I also saw that this white light functioned like a powerful laser, producing the entire G.o.D. scene, like a holographic display. The whole thing was vibrant and multi-dimensional (I got the sense there were 11 dimensions, but couldn't be sure since I didn't know what that even meant). Waves of light were flowing wildly and washing over the entire spirit-garden, beautifully joining all together into an oceanic expression of God's eternal goodness.

What a dazzling display of the masterful integration and orchestration of God's character traits, each one an expression of Their Divine Love.

I knew then that each interconnected spirit-being was identified by a unique and ever-changing fractal of these colors, as an ongoing expression of the life-giving and all-things-sustaining Breath of God. Somehow, God's breath-print within each spirit-being took the form of these wild yet intimate colors of Christ-expression. The breath of God, which is Their Life in us this very moment, apparently contains a personally crafted mix of these 100 trillion trillion colors flowing from Their prismatic light! De-light-full!!

CHAPTER 2: ILLUSTRATION – SANCTUARY OF THE DIVINE

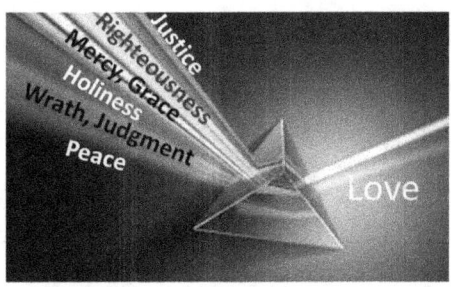

1 John 4:8-9 (AMPC)...for God is love. In this the love of God was made manifest (displayed) where we are concerned: in that God sent His Son, the only begotten or unique [Son], into the world so that we might live through Him.

The nature and character of God, as we see here, is unchanging and remains entirely consistent as the Story unfolds. Christ, the eternal Son, the same yesterday, today, and forever, shows us the essential nature of Divine Flow before man arrives on the scene. It is defined within the context of a perfect relationship, eternally shared within the Holy Community. We are all included as part of the One. There is no separation. And Love permeates the whole Garden ecosystem.

All we know about God's character begins here and lasts forever.

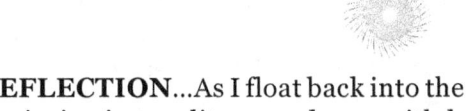

REFLECTION...As I float back into the awareness of my surroundings, this brain-jarring reality pounds me with break-necking force. I am in the center of the beautiful, mystical, interconnected Divine Flow in the vast color-soaked Garden of Delights. My identity is shaped by my union with the Divine and my connection to all the light-spirit-seeds that bear Their breath-print. Spirit, remind me that this identity will frame all of my moments as my life unfolds.

Creation has not yet begun, and I am surrounded by, marinating in, Love.

> ### Black Hole Takeaways from Pre-Creation
>
> - Christ is the Singularity in which the universe existed before Creation. And it is now sustained and held together in Him.
>
> - Our True Self is the Christ-Singularity deep within our inner universe, which is our spirit, entangled/joined with God and each other.
>
> - Spaghettification is the process by which the negative influences of body and soul are stripped away, and the True Self (Christ) can emerge as our real life.

As the scene before me started to fade, I fought to stay present. I didn't want to leave, but I knew I wasn't meant to stay. I let go reluctantly and felt myself floating away, slowly at first, then quickly picking up speed...Soon, I was hurtling through space, this time in the opposite direction.

Just as I was jettisoned out of our house and toward the black hole, I rocketed back through the ceiling and landed in my bed with a thunderous thud, staring wide-eyed at the ceiling, heart racing wildly. The last memory I had before leaving that pre-Creation scene, now rushing into my awareness, was that the whole Garden of Delights appeared to inhale and take a huge breath. I then had the strange feeling that the entire realm was about to give glorious birth...inside of me.

Before transitioning from the pre-Genesis Garden of Delights to a new Garden-the Garden of Eden-let's pause so I can share how this trip through the first black hole of Creation became a catalyst that helped frame my theology from an entirely different perspective. I'll call this model *Black Hole Theology*.

Chapter 3
Interpretation – A Wholesale Remodeling Project
(Topical)

Now THAT was a whole lot to take in, especially when I had no reference for much of what I saw, as it didn't fit within any boxes I previously had. A few of these observations came to the surface quickly and seemed important:

- The Christ-Singularity that contained the entire cosmos at the start of Creation.
- Our union with Christ and with each other.
- The universality of Christ's love for all who bear Their breath-print.
- The central reality of our spirit joined with God's Spirit as the core of our being.

Now, integrating these aspects into a coherent framework that included the best of both science and theology would take some time. I went off and began studying.

It took several years to find new clarity in my awareness, as dots started connecting between things I was studying in physics, psychology, neurology, theology, and church history. The Spirit began to weave a pattern as details began to mesh, and She started taking me through a massive reframe of my perspectives regarding reality. And to my surprise, what I thought was a "brand new" perspective echoed a historically *orthodox* view of faith present in the earliest segments of church history.

INTO THE ABYSS

Truth didn't change.

My understanding of Truth changed.

Before arriving at some of these details, my skeptical, over-analytical, intellect-oriented engineer mind wrestled for several years with concepts about God, various sacred scriptures, religious history, Greek and Hebrew word studies, and plenty of scholarly voices, especially in the fields of astrophysics and quantum mechanics. (To help with context, I've listed some resources at the end of the book.) The more I read and listened and studied, the more shocked and delighted I was at how much of my experience ran in perfect parallel to what our latest science was bringing to the forefront.

I finally came back to some semblance of structure for my "faith," as I realized that Truth couldn't change, but our understanding of it can and should be ever-changing as we learn and grow and mature along our journey. I also learned to trust that the Spirit would confirm and establish in me those things that were leading me in the right direction and burn away those that were based on my distortions and counterfeits. Yes, I had asked to be shown Reality, like a child approaching a heavenly Dad...but then I had to take the time to sit back, get quiet, and listen *as if I didn't already know the answers.*

As I said previously, I hold my opinions/beliefs quite loosely these days and always point folks toward the Spirit—the Voice above ALL other voices—as our greatest teacher in all these matters. Please don't take my word for it! Do your own research. I highly encourage Spirit-inspired curiosity and exploration. Keep this in mind as we look at a few beliefs that got a Black Hole Theology (B.H.T.) reframe.

Belief 1: The Bible – Inspiration vs. Inerrancy

We see the scriptures, not as THEY are, but as WE are.

> **Childhood Tradition:** Scripture is the inerrant, infallible, authoritative Word of God, and because it is the primary source of Truth and guidance for our lives, it should never be questioned. The Bible should be read as having been supernaturally delivered to us directly from God.

CHAPTER 3: INTERPRETATION – A WHOLESALE REMODELING PROJECT

>**Black Hole Reframe:** The scriptures are a library of books containing the inspired written accounts of a people growing in their understanding of the Divine. The authors wrote from their unique and sometimes differing perspectives, which requires us to enter the story and grapple with the texts, and perhaps more importantly, grapple with our own concepts of the Divine.

Jesus is the Word of God to Whom the scriptures are meant to lead us, which means that the Bible is pointing to a Reality greater than can be contained in a book. The Holy Spirit is our primary source of Truth and guidance, and questions are highly encouraged.

Scriptures and Humans are Both God-Breathed and Inspired

The Scriptures bear witness to humans as being all of the following: inspired; God-breathed; created in the image and likeness of God; knit together intricately by God in our mother's womb; fearfully and wonderfully made; vessels containing the very presence of God; having God's laws written on our hearts; joined with Christ in His death, burial, resurrection, and ascension; seated with Christ in heavenly places at the Father's right hand; holy, blameless, chosen in love before the foundation of the world; co-laborers with God; members of God's body on the earth.

Now given this impressive list, Paul is bold enough to refer to believers as "living epistles"...living letters or living scriptures, in other words. Wow! Just like Paul's letters were later compiled into what we know today as the Scriptures, at the time, he didn't realize that his written words would later be compiled and read by people across the entire world. He was simply writing letters to those he had met along the way. And he suggests, to our shock, that our lives and our words can be viewed as "living epistles," animated and inspired by God's very Spirit-breath... God-breathed living scriptures!

Yet, not a single person we know would likely ever look at the list above and claim that humans are inerrant (without a single error), infallible, and have the exact same authority as Christ does. After all, look at what happened with Adam. He was God-breathed and inspired, but he made quite a mess after he was created. "Inspiration" does not mean inerrancy, and it never has. The idea of "biblical inerrancy," in the way most understand it today, is a relatively new invention in church history.

INTO THE ABYSS

When the Roman Catholics assigned high authority and inerrancy to the Pope and church structure, the Protestants reacted by giving the same high authority and inerrancy to a book. A paper pope.

Inspired? Most definitely.

Inerrant? Most definitely NOT.

The inspired church and the God-breathed scriptures are only meant to lead us, through revelation and guidance from the Spirit, to Jesus. *He* is the actual inerrant, infallible, authoritative Word of God—the Logos/Logic of God manifested in time and space for us to see True Love expressed.

Bibliolatry is nearly impossible to detect because it masks as great respect. Yet quite unknowingly, we have made the Bible equivalent to God by assigning divine authority to it. As Jesus said to the religious leaders, "You search so diligently for eternal life in a book, but you refuse to come to Me, the source and sustenance of all life." And the apostle John opens his Gospel with this throwback to the Creation in Genesis: "In the beginning was the Word, and the Word was (face to face) with God, and the Word was God."

Don't settle for anything less than Christ as the object of your search in Scripture —He is the destination that your heart knows as its true home. The Scriptures merely point to God and are not themselves God. There are many voices in Scripture expressing thoughts and reflections regarding the Divine...but there's One Voice underneath, between all the words, drawing us toward Truth. This is the Voice we must actively listen for as we read—the quiet Voice leading us home.

> *"It is Christ Himself, not the Bible, who is the true word of God. The Bible, read in the right spirit and with the guidance of good teachers, will bring us to Him. We must not use the Bible as a sort of encyclopedia out of which texts can be taken for use as weapons."*
>
> **C.S. Lewis**[13]

---

13. Lewis, C S, and Walter Hooper. *The Collected Letters of C.S. Lewis*. San Francisco: Harper, 2004. Print. p. 247

CHAPTER 3: INTERPRETATION – A WHOLESALE REMODELING PROJECT

The Heavens Declare

Over half (57%) of the world doesn't have the Scriptures in their language, and many, many more are illiterate and couldn't read it even if they did. So here's a question: Is it possible that someone with no access to the Scriptures can know and experience God more deeply and intimately by observing the Creation than one who has full access to the Scriptures and ample study resources? Is God a respecter of persons, favoring the elite minority with a higher seminary education and access to nearly unlimited resources?

After all, Creation contains the "unfiltered" fingerprints of God, and those that studied the Scriptures most were also *so very wrong* about God's character when Jesus showed up on our planet.

This is worth our consideration.

The God Delusion

Here's a dangerous example of portraying the character of the Divine based on a literal, dead-letter, Spirit-lacking interpretation of specific Old Testament texts:

> *"The God of the Old Testament is arguably the most unpleasant character in all fiction: jealous and proud of it; a petty, unjust, unforgivable control-freak; a vindictive, bloodthirsty ethnic cleanser; a misogynistic, homophobic, racist, infanticidal, genocidal, filicidal, pestilential, megalomaniacal, sadomasochistic, capriciously malevolent bully."*
>
> **Richard Dawkins, Atheist - The God Delusion**[14]

At the core of this excerpt, Dawkins is calling his audience to reject this deity as fundamental fiction, in a wildly ironic twist. In contrast, Christian fundamentalists (like me for most of my life), who proudly wield an inerrant Holy Bible as a weapon to coerce beliefs and behaviors, call their audience to entrust their lives to this same deity. Why?

---

14. Dawkins, Richard, and OverDrive Inc. *The God Delusion*. Old Saybrook: Tantor Media, 2007.

Because according to the mainstream Christian model, God is sovereign and does whatever He pleases, even if what He pleases is grossly evil by His standards and morality definitions. Believing in these God-sanctioned activities—such as genocide, infant abuse, rape, abortion, killing people for disobedience, giving diseases to His children, etc.—essentially drains the term "godliness" of any credible meaning whatsoever.

Jesus is the perfect, complete revelation of God the Father, and Their character has NEVER changed. Perhaps the irony here is Dawkins *correctly* pointing out that a deity that doesn't look like Jesus…should be rejected.

Holy Spirit, paint for us inspired portraits of God's beautiful character, as revealed to us in Christ. May we never settle for a God Delusion.

Rorschach Test

The Bible is a deadly accurate Rorschach test, which the Spirit uses to penetrate and expose our hearts' thoughts and intents.[15] If you're not familiar, this psychological test is administered as a series of inkblots, and patients are asked to describe what they see. Of course, it's meant to tease the subconscious into revealing essential aspects of the person's soul. The inkblots don't change, but what people "see" is drastically different depending on their perspective, experience, and bias. It then gives the psychologist a basis to work from.

That's how it is with the Bible and with any other sacred text. We often see what we want to see and take away what we want to take, depending on our "lens." The *way* we read our scriptures is far more critical than *what* we read. It tells us more about us, about our perspective, than it does about God. When we interpret scripture, it's actually *reading us*, much to our amazement!

What we really need is a "secret decoder lens" to navigate the scriptures so that we can rightly divide the texts and discover Christ throughout the entire narrative. We learn this is possible in Luke 24, where Jesus had to teach His disciples how to properly read the Law, Prophets, and Writings in the Old Testament Scriptures. Jesus *is* that decoder lens, helping us to separate the stream of religion (based on man's misguided and fallen perspectives about God) from the stream of revelation (consistent with accurate views of God as found in Jesus), both of which run throughout the texts.

---

15. Choca, James. *The Rorschach Inkblot Test: An Interpretive Guide for Clinicians*. Washington, DC: American Psychological Association, 2013. Print.

CHAPTER 3: INTERPRETATION – A WHOLESALE REMODELING PROJECT

May our perceptions about God and ourselves line up with what God sees, so we can read and understand the scriptures in a way that leads us into the greater reality of Christ.

Belief 2: Why Did Jesus Come?

The lens through which we see Jesus is shaped by what we believe about ourselves.

> **Childhood Tradition:** Jesus came to die for our sins so that we could go to heaven when we die if we accept Him into our hearts. He took the Father's wrath, meant for us, upon Himself. He is our perfect, holy, and utterly unattainable example of living as a human.
>
> **Black Hole Reframe:** Jesus came to remind us of our original origin and identity in God and represents God's joining with all of humanity—our *At-One-Ment*. God in Christ reconciled the whole world to Himself, not counting men's sins against them. He is our perfect mirror. He shows us what's possible when living connected intimately to Abba, Who has eternally loved the whole world and always will. He also shows us the deadly patterns of violence and scapegoating that have been operating throughout our history, and invites us to consider a better way.

This part of my Black Hole reframe is quite simple, and I can cover it with three quotes. The first is from a beloved church mystic from the 1400s, and the next two are from contemporary authors who do an excellent job capturing the essence of this perspective. We'll dive further into the beauty of the Incarnation when we get to Part II.

Mothers of God

> *"What good is it to me if Mary gave birth to the Son of God 1400 years ago and I do not give birth to the Son of God in my own person and time and culture?...We are all meant to be mothers of God."*
>
> Meister Eckhart, German mystic[16]

Jesus Got Inside of Us

> *"The incarnation means He came inside your humanity and He sat inside your mental darkness. Inside your fears. He looked out through your eyes and said, 'I see what you see, but now let me tell you the truth,' and He tells you from the inside that His Father is your Father and He loves you with a fierce, perfect, everlasting love. And that, in fact, He not only loves, He IS love. You see, Jesus came down and got inside of us, and He got right down into the death that was ours... then He walked us out in resurrection and ascension. And He carried us home into the bosom of the Father where we belong."*
>
> Malcolm Smith, preacher and author[17]

Embracing the Whole Human Race

> *"It's not that believers are in and unbelievers are out... Jesus has embraced the human race and indeed, the entire cosmos. He's the one in and through and by whom it was all created, and*

---

16. Eckhart, Meister. Dum Medium Silentium, Sermon on Wisdom 18:14. See the Complete Mystical Works of Meister Eckhart, trans. And ed., Maurice O'C. Walshe (Crossroad: 2009), 29. Meister Eckhart also reflects on God and Mary as birthing Christ in Mandatum novum do vobis, Sermon on John 13:34. See Walshe, 427-430.

17. Smith, Malcom. Facebook post April 2016 https://www.facebook.com/BishopMalcolmSmith/

CHAPTER 3: INTERPRETATION – A WHOLESALE REMODELING PROJECT

now He's stepped into it and He's brought His relationship with the entire cosmos together in Himself, and given us a place in His relationship with the Father and with the Holy Spirit. That's who we are. That's our identity. We don't make that so. Whether we believe it or don't believe it doesn't change the fact of who we really are in Jesus."

C. Baxter Kruger, author and theologian[18]

Belief 3: End Times

We anticipate the future...not as IT is...but as WE are.

Childhood Tradition: There were signs all around us every moment of the world's end, all necessary to usher in events like the rapture, tribulation, millennial reign, and final judgment. There were, however, some disagreements on the details and timing of these events.

Black Hole Reframe: The book of Revelation is primarily about the Apocalypse—*the unveiling*—of God's character as the slain lamb, exemplified during Jesus' death on the cross. Much of the narrative describes historical events that happened in 70 AD with the Roman invasion and destruction of Jerusalem. However, the prophetic themes are incredibly relevant for us today, such as walking in the way of the Lamb amidst the dragons and beasts of our surrounding culture.

The Apocalyptic Revelation of Jesus Christ

Believers in first-century Palestine expected the arrival of a King that would enact a violent, bloody, Messianic overthrow and restore them to their rightful place before their enemies. They based their expectations on their honest, reverent, diligent study of their scriptures, coupled with a healthy awareness of the times and seasons.

---

18. Kruger, C. Baxter. An Inteview with C. Baxter Kruger, Feb. 2015. https://perichoresis.org/pages/interview-with-dr-baxter-kruger

INTO THE ABYSS

They got it completely,

Absolutely,

Wrong.

The justice they pictured involved sacrificing their enemies for their own benefit. They assumed God's justice was retributive, an eye for an eye, punishment to fit the crime.

Jesus is not planning on coming back to renounce the Sermon on the Mount and slaughter over 200 million people. Why would we think this about God? How could we?!

Rather than wholesale slaughter, Jesus came and demonstrated God's version of justice by sacrificing Himself for His enemies instead. He believed that Love would triumph and that His righteousness would *restore all* people to health and wholeness—to *shalom*. He loved the whole world, and this highlighted God's justice as restorative. It sets the world back to its original design.

This was a total and complete subversion of their expectation.

How about ours?

At the very least, keep open the possibility that mainstream expectations among modern believers for Jesus' "second coming" look very close to those of the religious leaders at His first coming. Just because we have more scripture doesn't mean that we don't see through the same distorted lens that they used.

We've been wrong before.
  We'll be wrong again.
    Humility is a very good idea . . .
      Let the Spirit lead you
        To a more beautiful portrait of Christ.

> **Rev. 1:1-2 (AMPC)** [This is] the revelation of Jesus Christ [His unveiling of the divine mysteries]. God gave it to Him to disclose *and* make known to His bond servants certain things which must shortly *and* speedily come to pass in their entirety. And He sent and communicated it through His angel (messenger) to His bond servant John, who has testified to *and* vouched for all that he saw [in his visions], the word of God and the testimony of Jesus Christ.

CHAPTER 3: INTERPRETATION – A WHOLESALE REMODELING PROJECT

The word **revelation** (Ἀποκάλυψις) in the Greek is "Apocalypse," and it means an "unveiling"...So our introduction is that we are about to read the *Unveiling of Jesus Christ*. More than the symbols, the timelines, and the detailed charts and graphs thousands have used to explain the book, the real intention is to throw back the curtains and show us the character of Jesus Christ as the central figure in the Grand Story.

I grew up embracing a futurist view of the book of Revelation; that it was a prophecy about how the end times were going to unfold. I assumed this was the only biblically faithful perspective. I didn't realize that this particular interpretation had come into popularity only recently in church history. I wasn't familiar with any alternative views that remained faithful and true to the scriptural texts.

Since childhood, my view was that there was only one particular way of seeing the end times, the mainstream framework since the mid-1800s. It involved a lightning-fast vacuum-like catching up (rapture) of the saints and an anti-Christ figure rising up during a tribulation period and wreaking utter havoc across the earth. This catastrophe would be followed (I was taught) by a holy army led by Jesus Himself that would wipe out His enemies with a sword, leaving rivers of blood in His wake. The only question in my understanding was the placement of the rapture and the millennium's details in context with the Great Tribulation (was it before, during, or after the Tribulation; i.e., pre-tribulation, mid-tribulation, or post-tribulation).

But how does this forecast align with the beautiful, universe-embracing-portrait of the crucified Christ we find before the Creation?

It doesn't.

Eventually, the narrative I grew up believing began to clash severely with my growing understanding of Christ's unconditional love for all people, including God's enemies. It also conflicted with the hope and desire Jesus spoke about regarding His expanding Kingdom. So I decided to take a deep dive into some serious study and found myself arriving at a *cross-infused perspective*. Here are four startling images in Revelation that forced me to reconsider the main themes of the book:

Subversion 1: The Roaring Lion is a Lamb.
There is an announcement of the Lion of the tribe of Judah. At face value, this reference to Christ corresponds to a mighty lion who rips apart his victims. However, this announcement

indicated that He had already overcome and conquered (before any ensuing battle occurred). In the vision, John then turns to see a little Lamb (not a Lion) as if it had just been slain (see Rev. 5:5-6). Yes, this One is undoubtedly a King, with all power and authority—but it's *how* He became King that is so shocking. This Ruler overcomes, not by might and power *over*...but by love and forgiveness and power *under*...This King is "the Lamb of God that takes away the sin of the world." From that point on, the Lion is no longer mentioned. Instead, the Lamb is mentioned 29 more times, thus making it the primary symbol as the narrative proceeds.

Subversion 2: The Robe is Bloody Before the Battle Begins.

The rider on the white horse is wearing a robe dipped in blood *before* He goes into battle against His enemies. It's not blood from His enemies—it's *His own blood*. It is another reference to the Lamb that was slain (see Rev. 19:13). Notice the constant, overarching theme throughout the narrative in Revelation.

Subversion 3: The Sword is Coming from His Mouth.

I'd always heard that Jesus was coming back with a sword, filled with a furious vengeance, to pierce through His enemies and spill their blood. I didn't realize the sword was coming from His mouth as He rides in on His stallion, robe already bloody (see Rev. 2:16, 19:15-21). Scripture aligns this reference to the sword of the Spirit—the Truth of God's Voice—which He uses to confront deception and judge the nations. This interpretation is a huge subversion to the common image of the sword in the first century. After this "fury of the wrath of God" is poured out, we find Jesus ruling over these same nations with righteousness and peace. This scenario isn't possible if He wipes them off the face of the earth!

Subversion 4: Saints Conquer by the Blood of the Lamb and Word of Their Testimony.

The theme continues around the example of the central Character. The Way of the Slain Lamb is the means to overcoming the enemy (see Rev. 20:4). It's quite humorous, actually...a tiny little Lamb wages war against the dragon and the beast with a sword of Truth and conquers them as the story moves forward.

CHAPTER 3: INTERPRETATION – A WHOLESALE REMODELING PROJECT

In this light, the Revelation of Jesus becomes a provocative guide to overcoming the enemy's anti-Christ systems through the power of cross-like love and mercy—the Love of the crucified and risen Lamb. It highlights the landscape into which the Gospel is meant to explode and expand.

Centering Criteria

I find that the centering criteria for all discussions on eschatology, the study of the last things, is the "portrait" our view paints of Christ.

The important questions aren't about particular views we have of the end times—whether they are theological positions like the futurist, preterist, historicist, or allegorical perspectives. The overarching question is whether the wrath, judgment, and holiness of God that we perceive is consistent with the Divine Flow we saw before the Creation, as well as in the incarnated life of God we find in the Gospel narratives.

More specifically, is it consistent with the Crucified Christ, where we most clearly see God's love expressed—an unconditional love that's fully and perfectly integrated with his wrath, judgment, holiness, and justice?

The book of Revelation is the Apocalypse, the "unveiling" of Jesus the Christ, who displays His Power as the Crucified and Risen and Victorious Lamb. Let's not distort the brilliant subversion by making it a literal book about "end times" and Anti-Christ figures and the necessity of God's Rambo-like bloody violence against Their enemies.

Let's emphasize our Beautiful God, the Crucified One Who joins Themselves to us to become our very life.

Belief 4: Afterlife

Our portraits of the afterlife are based primarily on who WE are.

> **Childhood Tradition:** Accept Jesus into your heart as Lord and Savior before you die, and eternity in heaven is your reward. Don't, and eternal conscious torment in hell is your fate. The endless fire of hell is God's righteous retribution against sinners, required by His infinite justice and holiness.

Black Hole Reframe: The all-consuming fire of God's holy love is both the torment of hell and the light of heaven, now and in the future, depending on one's posture toward the Divine. Ultimately, this fire is restorative, as God's mercy endures forever and Their love never fails.

HELL: A Fear-Fueled Foundation

The idea of "hell" as eternal conscious torment (ECT) after we die was one of the first of several dominoes to fall during my deconstruction. The vivid mental image of myself feasting at an eternal party while most of humanity, including loved ones and close friends, were screaming out in torment, grew to become a horrific, sickening thought to me.

What kind of God was I introducing people to follow, all in the name of "the Bible clearly says it, so it must be true"? Is He a moral monster that demanded our intimacy under threat of torture?! A deity that commanded us to love our enemies, while They planned all along to have Theirs endlessly tortured?!?

As I studied this out (which took over three years because of the respect I have for the Bible), I discovered other faithful ways to understand what the Scriptures were saying. I learned that the word "hell" as ECT was nowhere present, even as a Jewish concept, in the original texts. I was shocked to find out that four of the first six schools of theology in the early five centuries after Christ (Alexandra, Antioch, Caesarea, and Edessa/Nisbis) believed in the ultimate reconciliation of all people.

I also started to see how Jonathan Edwards' famous sermon "Sinners in the Hands of an Angry God" was one of the most influential messages in western Christendom. As such, it was the unspoken (or softly spoken) backdrop inside every church I had ever attended or visited. It vividly described the underlying motivation behind every evangelistic outreach, every service project, every prayer meeting, every children's program...all fueled by the "or else" of God's holy, fiery, excruciating wrath that would sustain folks forever in sheer torment if they didn't respond to Jesus in sincere love, and gain Their favor before it was too late.

CHAPTER 3: INTERPRETATION – A WHOLESALE REMODELING PROJECT

*"The God that holds you over the pit of hell,
much as one holds a spider, or some loathsome
insect over the fire, abhors you,
and is dreadfully provoked..."*
Jonathan Edwards[19]

This belief is a fictitious, fear-fueled foundation on which to build a movement of love. But what a brilliant mechanism to force a formulaic, transaction-based response, where the primary goal is to get people to say a sinner's prayer and cross a one-time salvation line so they can avoid hell torture.

Instead, let's embrace the tenacious solidarity of the Divine Community—with all of Creation bearing glorious witness. Let's help Their beloved image-bearers discover their True Selves and their unique place in the beautiful story and *apokatastasis* of God (the Greek term behind "the restoration of all things," as spoken in Acts 3:20-21).

A Holy and Horrific Hell

If we read the Bible using a flat and literal approach to inform our understanding of God's holiness and justice...

And if our interpretation requires us to believe in a place of eternal, conscious, nightmarish torture as God's holy punishment for those who don't recognize or return God's "unconditional" love while they are living on earth...

We MAY want to consider asking the Abba of Jesus about this perspective—then humbly and sincerely remain open to the possibility that we don't know every detail of the afterlife...

And wait expectantly for a response.

Many modern "theologies" feature a Freakish Finale (a deadly end to the Eternal Story that will include most of humanity) of grotesque and gruesome horror. It is a fear-based manipulation tactic meant to scare us into prayer-purchasing a post-mortem pyro-prevention policy.

---

19. Edwards, Jonathan, 1703-1758. Sinners In the Hands of an Angry God. A Sermon, Preached at Enfield, July 8, 1741, at a Time of Great Awakenings; and Attended with Remarkable Impressions on Many of the Hearers. By the Late Reverend Mr. Jonathan Edwards, President of the College of New-Jersey. New-York: Printed by G. Forman, opposite the post-office, for C. Davis, no. 94, Water-Street, 1797.

INTO THE ABYSS

Hell will force all its inhabitants to scream out in pain and terror, moment after moment, day after day, decade after decade, with not an ounce of relief. Followers of the Eternal Conscious Torment view hold to the necessity of this never-ending nightmare that makes the extremely worst of Hollywood's bloodiest horror films look like Disney World.

This is man's insatiable desire for God-sanctioned gratuitous vengeance at its very finest—or maybe it's very worst. These emotional "eye for an eye!" and "burn them alive!" themes of retributive violence run their evil course throughout human history.

Unfortunately, this is the dreadful mainstream backdrop of eternal hell torment against which God's message and unconditional love for the world (note: *without conditions*) is most often preached.

It's a deceptive "or else" message, attempting to provoke a terror-based response toward True Love. Even when not mentioned directly, it's positioned as the ever-present potential to end up a permanent prisoner in a haunted house of hellish horrors.

Horrifically Bad News for M O S T of us
　Is conveniently ignored because it's
　　Really Good News for only S O M E of us.

We should be cautious when our interpretation of scripture makes it impossible to distinguish between God's character and the character of evil dictators like Adolf Hitler or Emperor Nero. We might be following a counterfeit and believing a cleverly disguised demonic lie, all the while thinking we're simply faithful to the Bible.

We desperately need Christ to sanctify our imaginations (and motivate a humble, Spirit-guided reading of scripture) so that our theology can truly be consistent with God's eternal, relentless love for all those made in Their image.

Christ have mercy on us when we are so very certain of our scriptural perspectives, ones that often paint portraits of You that grieve Your beautiful heart.

Give us a more Glorious Vision.

CHAPTER 3: INTERPRETATION – A WHOLESALE REMODELING PROJECT

Show us Your True Nature,
  melt away the counterfeits and
    distortions, and unveil Your Beauty.
Make us experiential witnesses of a violent Divine Love
  and a raging Eternal Mercy that destroy any demonic notions
    of a holy and just torture chamber.

The Logic of Line-Crossing: Satan vs. God

Does someone have to ask Satan into their heart to enter hell when they die? I had never considered this scenario for most of my life.

Why are we told we need to specifically ask Jesus into our heart to cross over a "line in the sand" and gain salvation, but the devil can possess anyone, anytime, without any permission? Let's think about our logic here. Have we naively reduced the entirety of the Gospel down to a line-crossing mandate to avoid torture? How many times growing up did I hear the gently spoken but ominous threat, "If you died tonight, do you know where you'd spend eternity?"

Well, suppose Satan ultimately triumphs in the end, *dragging a vast majority of humanity into endless torment* (according to mainstream evangelical theology). In that case, I guess it makes sense that when you peek behind the "Wizard-of-Oz salvation curtain," the evangelical model of the Gospel *requires* Satan to be more powerful than God.

Of course, many Christians would vehemently disagree with this controversial statement. They quickly remind us that they continuously worship their All-Mighty God...while being fully persuaded that Satan will successfully convince most people to join him in hell forever at the close of human history.

So...

The gates of "hell"
  Prevail in the end
    For most everyone
      Who has ever lived?!?

There is a *much different and better way* to see God than this.

Love God or Else

Forced sexual intimacy
  With another person
    Under threat of severe pain
      And agonizing torture if they don't comply
     All while whispering words
       Of sincere, authentic love in their ear…

  Is *Physical Rape*
    I think we can agree.

Forced intimate relationship
  With God
    Under threat of eternal, conscious
     Agonizing torment if they don't comply
     All while whispering words
      Of unconditional love in their ear…

  Is *Spiritual Rape*
    I hope we can consider this thought together.

"Love will never invoke fear.
  Perfect Love expels fear,
    Particularly the fear of punishment.
  The one who fears punishment
Has not been completed through love."
I John 3 (VOICE)

CHAPTER 3: INTERPRETATION – A WHOLESALE REMODELING PROJECT

Certainty about the Afterlife

A final thought...In the area of our beliefs where we don't and can't know for certain (only One knows for sure), we throw ourselves and those we love into the impossibly wide arms of God's forever-enduring mercy. Their eternal and unfailing keeping-no-record-of-wrongs love and Their relentless, burning desire that all of Their image-bearers would ultimately experience Them as Source, Sustenance, and Salvation.

And yes, this mercy, love, and desire are perfectly and wholly integrated with Their holiness, justice, and wrath. Remember here the glorious prismatic effect when the pure white light of God's Love illuminated the cross, bursting forth into those 100 trillion trillion colors, representing all the perfectly orchestrated aspects of Their character.

We have an eternally beautiful God. And we can trust what we experientially know about God's beautiful character with the details of the afterlife.

Framing the Reframe: Starting Point and Vantage Point

All of these emerging perspectives were framed by discovering the Christ-Singularity as the starting point, and Their Love for all humanity as the vantage point for all things theological and practical. We miss so much when we don't start our story back in the beginning, in Genesis chapter 1 as opposed to Genesis 3. And actually, we need to start in the pre-beginning!

After seeing certain portraits of God from my time in the pre-Creation Garden...well, there are some things that once you see, you can never unsee. This became especially true as I started seeing modern science so clearly and consistently laying out its clues and confirmations regarding God's beauty.

I first thought I had found a "brand new" theology, but it ended up looking a whole lot like what the original church fathers believed and taught. I found myself resonating with the words of G.K. Chesterton, who, in his classic book *Orthodoxy* wrote, "I did try to found a little heresy on my own; and when I had put the last touches to it, I discovered that it was orthodoxy." [20]

As I said before, I would highly encourage you to ask hard questions, to study some of these things on your own. Wander outside of your echo chamber to seek those who have experience apart from your tradition, and then trust the Holy Spirit to guide you into Truth. We are all on a journey,

---

20. Chesterton, G K. Orthodoxy. Garden City, N.Y: Image Books, 1959.

and God meets us exactly where we are in the moment. I believe it's also best to hold our "beliefs" loosely, because all of us are more wrong than we realize about certain things!

These days, I have never loved the scriptures more, because I finally saw the Greater Reality they were pointing us toward—Christ—the Singularity, our Sustaining Reality, the Love that holds the whole universe together. If the scriptures are a jigsaw puzzle, then Jesus is the image on the cover, pointing us to an even greater reality that He came to put on display.

When we understand we are one with the Hero of the Story—and when we know that Their love will not fail in the end—our perspectives about our lives are bound to transform.

> ### Black Hole Takeaways from the Reframe
> - The starting point of man's story is our *actual* union with God (Genesis 1-2) instead of our *perceived* separation from God (Genesis 3).
> - Our vantage point for everything—from theology, to cosmology, to anthropology—is God's love for the entire world, as shown on the cross.
> - The Spirit is free to guide us into truth when we ask honest questions (as if we don't already know the answers).

Chapter 4
Integration – Bookends of the Story
(Genesis 1 and Revelation 22)

At the end of my black hole experience, I anticipated the glorious birth of the cosmos. But before we look at this together, let's jump briefly to *the end* of the Story. You might think, why so soon? Won't it ruin the "punchline" if we read the ending already? Trust me, we'll be OK. The bookends of the Story will help provide a clear context for everything in the middle. Plus, we already know what happens. Love wins in the end! Oops...punchline is on the table!

When we zoom forward in time, we discover another cosmic phenomenon at the end of the story, featuring an enormous force toward its center, exactly like we witnessed at the beginning of time when I was swept into a black hole. Just as the entire universe was contained in the Christ-Singularity at the moment of creation, we find the same substantial universe-wide gravitational force drawing everything everywhere toward its destination at the Story's grand finale. As mentioned before, this was known throughout church history as the "apokatastasis," referring to the restoration of all things.

The same Love that set Creation in motion is now drawing the cosmos toward a wondrous ending.

Christ is the Alpha-point at the dawn of First Creation, and Christ is the Omega-point as the New Creation is being ushered into existence. We've been given a vision of the story's "ending" in the book of Revelation:

> Rev. 21:3-6 (AMPC) Then I heard a mighty voice from the throne, *and* I perceived its distinct words, saying, "See! **The abode of God is with men, and He will live (encamp, tent) among them; and they shall be His people, and God shall personally be with them and be their God.** God will wipe away every tear from their eyes; and death shall be no more, neither shall there be anguish (sorrow and mourning) nor grief nor pain anymore, for the old conditions *and* the former order of things have passed away." And He Who is seated on the throne said, "See! I make all things new." Also, He said, "Record this, for these sayings are faithful (accurate, incorruptible, and trustworthy) and true (genuine)." And He [further] said to me, "It is done! I am the Alpha and the Omega, the Beginning and the End. To the thirsty, I [Myself] will give water without price from the fountain (springs) of the water of Life."

The Divine, Dancing Flow of Love that we glimpsed in the pre-Creation was extended in the physical realm to those with eyes to see and ears to hear this Reality. And this scene never ends. The beauty of this fellowship is no longer constrained by time as we know it. In the end, God lives with and in those They have always loved. The entire universe is being drawn toward this stunning conclusion as we speak.

Now, we recognize, of course, that much happens between the Beginning and the End...much indeed! This drama unfolds with all the fantastic elements that make it such a compelling read. It encompasses villains and deception, conquests and betrayals, daring rescues and vicious hatred, amazing grace, and incredible pain. The Story captivates us with hope and faith and debilitating despair, undeniable truth, and impossibly terrible decisions, natural failures, and supernatural acts that defy all logic, the ongoing war between good and evil, culminating with the ultimate triumph of good in the end. We'll get to some of that shortly.

However, let's not lose sight of the Story, the Christ-Story, unfolding before us. The Story is "book-ended" by two black hole realities, and we can't bypass these Alpha and Omega scenes too quickly, or we'll miss the essence filling in the gap between them like I did for most of my life. Yes, without clearly knowing the bookends of our story, we will almost certainly ignore the trajectory in which we find ourselves at this very moment—from pre-Creation to New Creation.

CHAPTER 4: INTEGRATION – BOOKENDS OF THE STORY

We aren't supposed to try and fit God into our tiny, individual stories. God has designed reality so we can only find our True Selves when we allow Them to include us into the great, eternal Story, the Story above all stories, the drama of the ages. It's the beautiful Story of God, and we're going to discover that every single one of us has a unique role to play in bringing it to this glorious end. The Faithful One that set the whole thing into motion is working in and through Their Creation to complete what They began. Christ isn't only an observer at the start and close of the story...Christ IS the Beginning and the End, the Alpha and the Omega. Now that's a confidence booster if I've ever known one!

OK, we have our bookends now—two slices of cosmic black hole bread for our Christ-Story sandwich! Let's transition from the pre-beginning Sanctuary of the Divine and make our way slowly to the edge of Creation... from the Garden of Delights to the Garden of Eden.

Ready?

Chapter 5
Inspiration – Creation, the Original Scriptures
(Genesis 1-2)

"This most beautiful system of the sun, planets and comets, could only proceed from the counsel and dominion of an intelligent and powerful Being."

Isaac Newton[21]

Love's Explosion

Remember the psycho-insane gravitational pull into a black hole, from which not even light can escape? The energy and mass of a billion suns imploding into a dot that can fit on the tip of a needle? The phenomenon that makes the latest science-fiction look like archaic animation?

Imagine now a black hole in reverse, spilling and spewing, spinning and spitting out its contents at light speed, flinging them into the farthest reaches of fathomless space. Infinity erupts from within itself and unleashes a new form of Reality. A black-hole-in-reverse is what astrophysics calls a white hole.

I picture this incredible beauty the moment God speaks into existence the entire cosmos *in Christ,* utilizing the authority of Their speaking voice to express what was within Them to form the projection of all that is. The whole universe existing within the Christ-Singularity, the essence of pure Love contained within

---

21. Newton, Isaac, 1642-1727. Newton's Principia : The Mathematical Principles of Natural Philosophy. New-York: Daniel Adee, 1846.

INTO THE ABYSS

the Garden of Delights, now becomes the ultimate explosion from within the depths of the Divine. Their Story now begins to take shape in the new "dimensions" of space and time, matter, energy, and frequencies, all sustained within the same Divine Consciousness (the mind of Christ) present before the Creation.

> *"If you want to find the secrets of the Universe, think in terms of energy, frequency, and vibration."*
> **Nikola Tesla**[22]

The vision of the Godhead, the dream that found its birthplace in the pre-beginning, is now unfolding. The worlds are purposely flung into existence, the earth and skies and seas flooded with exquisite beauty and intricate detail. Features, creatures, and flora of every exuberant variety are joyfully fashioned to bring hints of the Creator into every corner of the globe. God's explosive creation is planting Divine seeds of eternity into every subatomic particle that comprises the universe.

Though we might affirm that God created "ex nihilo" (out of nothing), we know the One Who contains, gives birth and sustains the Creation was and is Christ. At its core, creation is a Divine universe-creating orgasm, seeding the entire realm of time and space with the essence of Christ that joins the whole universe together within Themselves. Imagine the universe as a *black hole turned inside out*—a Singularity that has issued forth all that exists.

Love has exploded!!

> **John 1:2-3 (VOICE)** This *celestial* Word remained ever-present with the Creator; His speech shaped the entire cosmos. *Immersed in the practice of creating,* all things that exist were birthed **in Him**.

> **Col. 1:16-17 (AMPC)**...all things were created *and* exist through Him [by His service, intervention] **and in *and* for Him**. And He Himself existed before all things, and **in Him all things consist** (cohere, are held together).

---

22. Tesla, Nikola. Conversation with Ralph Bergstresser, 1942.

CHAPTER 5: INSPIRATION – CREATION, THE ORIGINAL SCRIPTURES

REFLECTION... Spirit, paint a picture in my soul of the moment the Voice spoke it all into existence—when eternity exploded, and the universe began to take shape. Put me inside the Christ-Singularity and make me an eyewitness to God's orgasmic Creation the instant it began. Fill me with the wonder of Creation's birth and the entangled universe that arose as a result.

Our Connection with the Creation

If we could "see" in super-slow motion what was taking place down at the subatomic level as the universe was formed, we would experience the wonder of entanglement between all the particles that first existed inside the Christ-Singularity. As said before, this is the quantum field that is now permeating the expanding universe. We would see this energy field as an all-encompassing ocean, and all other created things as waves that rise and find their form within it. The beauty of this interconnected reality—entanglement—will have profound effects later on as we find our place in the Story. When we see how closely we are connected at the subatomic level to all other things in existence, a boatload of new possibilities suddenly appear on our radar.

In the last several decades, certain experiments, initially dismissed as "pseudoscience," are seeing a resurgence within the emerging framework of quantum physics. The experiments themselves weren't at fault for being ignored—they were well-planned, controlled tests by credentialed scientists in their fields of expertise. The issue was that they had no cohesive framework to explain what they were seeing; therefore, the experiments were often shunned by the broader scientific community. However, recent advances in quantum physics have supplied us with a new framework and a new way of seeing. The result is a game-changing adjustment to the way we observe our universe.

Here is a cluster of fascinating examples that show us the deep levels of connection we share with all of Creation...in Christ. I've included several references at the end of the book for further study, so I'll limit these to brief overviews of the experiments that were conducted.

- In the mid-1990s, Japanese scientist Masaru Emoto showed that water responds to thoughts, pictures, and prayers by forming different crystal patterns when it was frozen.[23]
- Cleve Baxter, a former CIA interrogator, got the idea of hooking up plants to a "lie detector" machine and demonstrated that plants immediately responded when he *thought* of doing damage to them. He showed the same

---
23. Emoto, Masaru. *Hidden Messages in Water*, Atria Books; September, 2005, Later Printing ed.

results with many different plants, yogurt bacteria, eggs, and human sperm. He called this phenomenon "primary perception" and claimed it could be measured in all living things, hypothesizing that they can *sense* pain and affection.[24]

- Scientist David Wilcock cites hundreds of little-known but peer-reviewed scientific experiments, all demonstrating the *consciousness of various types of matter* and its connection to everything else.[25]
- *Secret Life of Plants* is a documentary that shows plants exhibiting the following behaviors demonstrating their own consciousness:[26]
    - Plants communicate among themselves to spread information, such as potential danger.
    - Sagebrush cooperated with other branches of itself to avoid being eaten by grasshoppers.
    - A Russian experiment with two cabbage plants demonstrated that when one plant was hooked to a machine with electrodes, its energy frequencies were converted into audible tones. The other cabbage, which was *not* hooked to any instrument, was then randomly harmed. While this happened, the plant hooked to the machine was heard "crying" or "screaming" in harsh high-pitched tones.
    - A man in a controlled experiment was asked to watch a series of film clips of random events—from kids playing to bombs destroying villages—while he was hooked to a polygraph machine. The plant next to the man also hooked to an identical machine, mirrored the needle movements on the man's graph paper, indicating a change of "emotion" to the same energetic vibrations.
    - These authors, through an extensive series of experiments, portrayed the sentient quality of common plants. Rather than some wacko theory, this is simply the natural result inside the framework of a quantum field of energy, the backdrop being a Divine Consciousness from which all things have their existence. All of Creation is connected in Christ, and the implications require us to set aside our ideas of clearly marked lines of separation…to look with our eyes wide open at what the quantum field is showing us about our world and our place within it.

---

24. Baxter, Cleve, International Journal of Parapsychology: "Evidence of a Primary Perception in Plant Life," vol. 10, no. 4, pp. 329-348, Winter 1968.
25. Wilcock, David. *The Source Field Investigations*. New York: Dutton, 2011.
26. Tompkins, Peter; Bird, Christopher. *The Secret Life of Plants*. New York: Perennial, 1989.

CHAPTER 5: INSPIRATION – CREATION, THE ORIGINAL SCRIPTURES

OK. What's all this talk of Divine consciousness and a universal field of energy? And why does it matter? I can imagine a few eye rolls and looks of concern that we're now off in the theological weeds. We're simply placing the phrase "in Christ" on the table—it is used generously throughout the New Testament Scriptures—and then looking closely at what it means in the context of black holes and the resulting quantum field that emerged from the Creation event.

According to Einstein's famous equation $E=MC^2$ (or mass = energy divided by the speed of light squared), energy and mass are interchangeable. They are different forms of the same thing. Matter is simply *energy vibrating at different frequencies*. This is because all matter was originally resident inside the same Source—Christ—and made of the same basic building blocks. This conclusion doesn't depend on the state of energy, whether solid, liquid, gas, or plasma, or whether it shows up as a human, animal, plant, or simple organism.

Max Planck, physicist and co-founder of quantum mechanics, said, "All matter originates and exists only by virtue of a force which brings the particles of the atom to vibration. I must assume that behind this force, is the existence of a conscious and intelligent Mind. This Mind is the matrix of all matter."[27] Note that he's not only saying that there is an intelligent consciousness as the force *behind* matter...he's also saying that this intelligent consciousness *is* the matter, implying that any concept of separation between created and Creator is merely an illusion.

There is an ocean of energy that flows throughout everything on our planet, our solar system, our entire universe. This invisible energy field ties all of Creation together—people, plants, pets, peninsulas, and planets. All of it is manifested forms of energy (matter) that are intricately connected and entangled together. Supplying order, meaning, and direction to this ocean of energy is a Divine Consciousness, the mind of Christ. Mystics across many faith traditions have been able to see and experience this interconnectedness in all things—in other words, our Oneness in Christ. In essence, the entire universe functions as a sentient organism. The entire Creation in a very real sense is the "Incarnation" or the "Body" of Christ.

As described in Colossians and other scriptures, this "in-Christ-ness" of all things in the Creation, beginning to end, is the context we'll work within as we move forward from here.

---

27. Planck, Max. 1944. "Das Wesen der Materie" ("The Nature of Matter"), speech delivered in Florence, Italy: Archiv zur Geschichte de Max-Planck-Gesellschaft, Abt. Va, Rep. 11 Planck, Nr. 1797.

Why Create?

Creation is our original "sacred text," the first raw and unfiltered testament of God, as seen in the physical form of all things. The first tangible evidence we have of God's beauty and wisdom and creativity and love is expressed into the entire cosmos. We need to dive into this mystery with eyes and ears wide open so that we can find ourselves as active participants in this Story…we the Body, Christ the Head.

Why did God create? Why risk ruining a perfect existence shared within the pre-Creation Garden of Delights? It's certainly not out of any need, because God has no need or lack. God only has desire, which is born from the immensity of Their shared flow of love, to create.

As the Creation account reaches its culmination in Genesis, God-in-Three is about to extend Their fellowship by fashioning a creature made in Their very image and likeness. There's too much Love to keep to Themselves! It's about to overflow and become an extended family. The force of the Cosmos has initiated a love-driven trajectory moving the Story forward, and we will get a good glimpse in the opening scenes of how humanity enters this new realm of time and space…and choice.

Adam: Humanity is Born

It would serve us well to imagine this spectacular interaction. The final act of the Creation is before us. Lean in…draw close…

See God's tenderness expressed as They affectionately fashion from dust the first one made for intimacy; the innocent one who would be hand-crafted in Their image and likeness. Savor the wonder of the Creator's breath as They infuse Their very Spirit-life into Their masterpiece and animate it as a living being…the first human soul. Picture a universe-filling "gasp" as the Three-in-Love behold Their handiwork, Their self-sculpture…and offer a blessing over it, declaring with joy that it is "very good." Take in Their joy unspeakable as man receives a role in the Creation, to care for his world, to multiply and fill it to extend the Creator's loving presence and oversight to the ends of the earth.

This is an amazing scene, the first time in Creation that the universe has become self-aware. God's breath + dust of the ground = a Divine image-bearer that is aware of itself as a living, breathing soul.

CHAPTER 5: INSPIRATION – CREATION, THE ORIGINAL SCRIPTURES

Elements of Garden Life

When we see God for who They are and visualize Their dream for Creation, we begin to discover more of who *we* truly are. Are we able to see the Divine Flow here and our inclusion into Their vision for the world? This is even more relevant for us when we see that "Adam" is from the Hebrew word representing humanity, and "Eve" is from the word meaning the mother of all living. Here were some of the dynamics taking place in the Garden:

- ***Intimate Union:*** Everything in the Original Paradise flowed from the intimacy of union that God shared with Adam and Eve.

- ***Lavish Provision:*** Every provision, every pleasure that man could desire, was given freely to enjoy.

- ***Loving Prohibition:*** God set a boundary around the Tree of Knowledge of Good and Evil, prohibiting them to eat of it, to avoid the taste of pain and judgment that came from embracing a false identity.

- ***Meaningful Work:*** Man was given specific tasks as God's expressions, caring for and ruling over Their Creation.

- ***Deep Sense of Purpose:*** The Story was heading somewhere, and mankind was given a pivotal role to move Creation forward toward its ultimate fulfillment.

Inside Adam, Inside Humanity

Let's pause here and peer within the first man. After all, humanity in its entirety was in Adam's loins at the time, so it's helpful for us to explore this intimate interaction between Creator and created. True to form, God-in-Three fashions a three-part Creation, formed in Their own image and likeness. Just as They had dreamed, heaven kisses earth and we emerge from the dust.

> **Gen. 2:7 (NLT)** Then the Lord God formed man from the dust of the ground (***body***) and breathed into his nostrils the breath (***spirit***) of life, and man became a living being (***soul***).

Entire volumes have been written on this topic of spirit, soul, and body. That said, we'll condense it down to the following as we frame the concept of man's identity:

INTO THE ABYSS

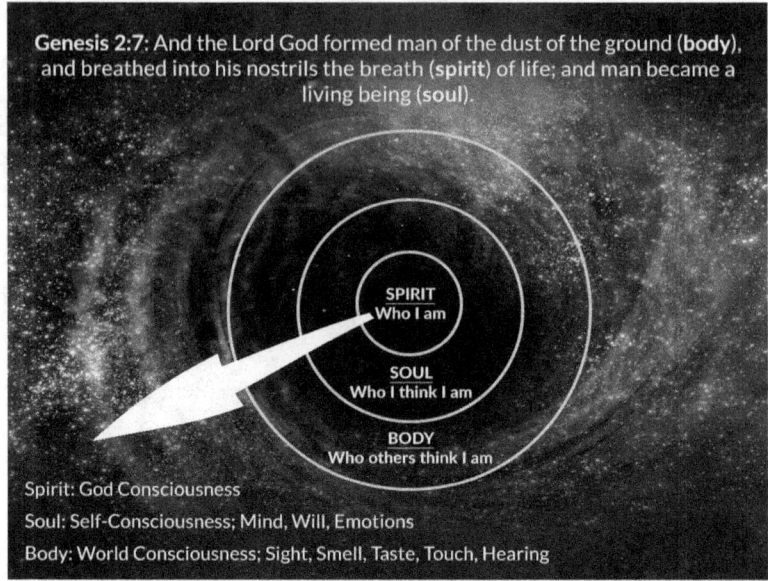

IDENTITY MODEL: SPIRIT, SOUL, AND BODY

Every man's innermost being (spirit) contains a black hole Singularity (a wormhole) that joins us directly to the Divine. These marvelous, magical realities of the galaxies are found in outer space, and also the deep, incredible inner universe within each of us. God's very Spirit-breath is our life, the central reality that animates us and allows us to be aware of our own existence.

> **1 Cor. 6:17 (NLT)** But the one who joins himself to the Lord is one spirit with Him.

We were created to live from the inside out, finding identity and life from the union our spirit shares with the infinite Spirit of Christ within. When we become aware of the infinite God (spirit) as the Source and Center of our being, we form our personality and core beliefs (soul) based on this awe-filled awareness of union with the Divine. Then, we can physically express this Reality to the world around us (body). In this way, we join the Creator in expressing Their love, joy, and peace toward the whole of Creation. This was the vision of God laid out in the first two chapters of Genesis.

If we look closely, we might see that Eden's garden is a picture of our human soul, the place where we can experience tangible communion with the Divine. Remember the Garden of Delights in the pre-Creation realm, where all of our interconnected spirits enjoyed union with God? Now, we see that when Spirit

CHAPTER 5: INSPIRATION – CREATION, THE ORIGINAL SCRIPTURES

enters a body and a soul is formed, this inner soul-garden within us is where we can *enjoy* the reality that our spirits are continually experiencing in and with God. It's where our mind, emotions, and will participate in the Divine Flow taking place each moment deep within us, which can then overflow as Presence-based thoughts, feelings, beliefs, and decisions within our lives.

Eyes Wide Open

Consider the breathtaking image that the first man enjoyed when he opened his eyes for the very first time...God-of-All-Creation, kneeling before Adam in adoration and joy, beholding Their masterpiece after a life-giving kiss. This moment—this essential breath of life—signals that humanity was designed to receive this reality from our Maker. We are to "open our eyes" (so to speak) as we awaken for the first time and see the eternal eyes of God, beholding us with adoring love, affirming what They had made as "very good," sharing Their life-breath with us.

This...is Gospel. Good News. Original Blessing!

Can we picture Adam's sheer amazement here?

Heaven kisses earth and Adam emerges from the dust...*We* emerge from the dust...wholly formed to find our life and sustenance within the sanctuary of God. The Divine fellowship is extended by one, soon to be two, with the intention for them to "multiply and fill the earth." God and man enjoy fellowship in the cool of the day, walking in the deep intimacy available when there is One source of love and life.

This is paradise in every tangible sense of the word. Man is gently drawn into the Divine Sanctuary of truth, and love and freedom, hand-crafted and sent forth after God pronounces Their handiwork, Their masterpiece, to be very good. The original Hebrew text in Genesis 2 suggests that God kneels in adoration before Adam as though gazing into a mirror.

This is where we find the Source of our awe and our innocence.

REFLECTION...As God kneels in the dirt and breathes Their Spirit into Their image-bearing self-sculpture, I put myself behind Adam's eyes as he opens them for the first time. What do I sense when I behold God's eyes fixed on me with delight and adoration? My soul is open, and I will drink this slowly.

INTO THE ABYSS

The Voice

*The entire Cosmos
is presently screaming
to its inhabitants
about their Creator,
and about Their
Divine Origin
in Christ.*

*But many other voices
compete
for our attention.
Loud and convincing
voices.
The Voice
behind all other voices
is not deterred
in the least.*

*In fact,
any unbiased
exploration of the Universe
will lead any honest seeker
to witness the
fingerprints of Spirit,
and hear the invitation
in Her Beautiful Voice.*

"Come Home"

CHAPTER 5: INSPIRATION – CREATION, THE ORIGINAL SCRIPTURES

All is well, and everyone lived happily ever after...no, wait.

Wait a second.

There's a famous movie that capitalizes on the audience's primal fears by using a two-note *ostinato,* or a repeating musical motif. If I played it now, nearly everyone would recognize it immediately. It's the reason why the composer won his first of 22 Grammy awards. I'm referring to the theme from the movie *Jaws* when the Great White is about to make its appearance.[28] It's such a primitive, simple motif, but it seems to tap into something deep in our subconscious mind and remain lodged there. In our Story, we might imagine something approaching our event horizon... something...sinister.

We might hear this famous orchestral riff in the background, now. *Baaaahhh Dumm. Bah Dum.* Can you hear it? Alas, our Story, as with all fantastic stories, will soon take a terrible, troubling twist toward treachery and treason.

We will soon discover how easily we are made vulnerable by enemy attack.

The villain is about to make an appearance in our Great Story.

Black Hole Takeaways from the Creation

- The "in-Christ-ness" of the entire God-whispered universe is a way of saying that everything remains connected and joined together (entangled) within the field of energy that permeates the Cosmos, starting at the Creation moment.

- The creation of Adam (humanity) and Eve (mother of all living) represents *all of us* as God-breathed, inspired creations.

---

28. Jaws. Directed by Stephen Spielberg, Music by John Williams, USA, 1975.

Chapter 6

Infestation – Something Sinister This Way Slithers

(Genesis 3)

We see God, not as THEY are, but as WE are.

We are *not* separated from a holy God because of our sin. Separation from God *would* equal *non-existence*. The only thing that "separates" us from God is the *thought* that we are separate from God, and even our thoughts don't *actually* separate us; they only deceive us into believing an untruth.

"What comes into our minds when we think about God is the most important thing about us...For this reason, the gravest question before the Church is always God Himself, and the most portentous fact about any man is not what he at a given time may say or do, but what he in his deep heart conceives God to be like. **We tend by a secret law of the soul to move toward our mental image of God.** This is true not only of the individual Christian, but of the company of Christians that composes the Church. Always the most revealing thing about the Church is her idea

INTO THE ABYSS

of God, just as her most significant message is what she says about Him or leaves unsaid, for her silence is often more eloquent than her speech."

A. W. Tozer[29]

Every epic story has an epic villain.

The Poisonous "IF"

The enemy sneaks into the story as an evil spirit of deception, using a talking snake's imagery. This infamous serpent successfully inserts a strategically placed "if" into the equation set into place by God Himself. "*If* you want to be like God, then…" But remember, according to Genesis 1:26, God-in-Three had **already** fashioned Eve and Adam to be like Them, **already** created the first humans in God's very image and likeness to enjoy intimate love within the Trinitarian flow. Adam and Eve **already** bore the stamp of eternity. They were the objects of Divine Love, enjoying the beauty of sweet fellowship in their garden paradise. Their souls were deeply satisfied with the loving provisions and prohibitions of intimate relationships with God and each other.

Truth – We're in union with our Creator, animated by God's Spirit, joined to the Divine as an INTERNAL reality.

Lie – We're separate from God, and there is something EXTERNAL to us that we need, to bridge the gap.

In the Garden of Eden, a poisonous "IF" (let's call this the *PoisIF*) found a way into our minds and hearts, and its effects included feelings of separation, darkness, fear, confusion, shame, and uncertainty. Do you see it? Eden is an image of our soul-garden—the place of our self-consciousness where our personality dwells, and our beliefs form—and the serpent of deception is ever-present. The height of this soul deception is an often-successful attempt to convince us that we are separate from God and each other.

The story shows us what happens as we **reorient and filter how we perceive God** so that other options become attractive. When this *PoisIF* gets inside us, we become convinced we must seek "life" and "identity" *outside* of the affirmation, shalom, and pleasure that God alone provides.

---

29. Tozer, A.W. *Pursuit of God; Knowledge of the Holy* Amazon.com Services LLC, Nov 28, 2013.

CHAPTER 6: INFESTATION – SOMETHING SINISTER THIS WAY SLITHERS

This killer toxin then soaks the fertile soil inside our soul-garden, out of which fruits of violence, pain, and destruction grow and manifest. Yes, this poisonous, fertile soil is evident as we look across the separation-soaked landscapes of our world today. We have ingested the poisonous "IF," and it has done precisely what the Fraud had anticipated.

It has kept us from discovering the truth about God, about ourselves, and our deep connection to each other, in Christ.

As we continue to operate within the great deception, making it our own, we look right past the invitation into the grand Trinitarian Dance. In our deep confusion, we attempt to suck life and identity from multiple alternatives apart from our Creator.

Reversal of the Inside-Out Design

Before Genesis 3, Adam and Eve seemed to lack nothing in the garden. They were in an ideal situation in which to mature and grow in Truth. The original paradise! They experienced everything God had dreamed for those created in Their image and likeness—intimate and authentic relationship, lavish provision, divine health, beautiful surroundings, deep purpose. Reality in the story was that Adam and Eve were the objects of God's eternal affection, living in perfect love and freedom, participating fully within the Godhead's life. If anyone could claim "having it all," it would be them. Eden's soul-garden, from all appearances, looked like it should have been a picture of inner peace and harmony...but it wasn't enough.

Again, the lie presented by the enemy spirit found its weight by introducing the subtle possibility that a holy, separated God did not really have their best interest in mind. When they believed this, it blinded them to the truth about God's infinite love as well as the truth about themselves as the recipients of that love. Now, instead of living in an environment founded in trust and freedom, they believed that God was withholding something that would *really* make them free, fulfilled, and able to trust completely. Perhaps this wasn't the first time they had considered this possibility? They were questioning God's goodness. They were wondering about their true identity.

Remember how God designed Adam as a three-part being, meant to live from the inside out? This design was reversed by the introduction of the *PoisIF* and the possibility of "outside-in" living. This involved a *perceived* identity influenced by external sources instead of by its intimate connection to the Divine Flow. This externally driven identity is what led humanity down a dangerous path toward violence, addictions, religious certainty, pain, and death . . .

Consequences in the Soul-Garden

There were consequences for believing and acting on the deception that what they had was somehow not enough; that God was holding out on them, and that they were separate from Him.

1. The first and deadliest consequence is that they were no longer able to see God accurately. They immediately perceived that God had changed, so they ran away and hid, covering their fear and guilt and shame with fig foliage. The *PoisIF* virus had severely altered their vision. They now "saw" a god that they thought was furious and frightening—an image projected through their own newly found filter of shame. Through this false filter, they perceived God as separate from them, filled with wrath, and out for punishment.

   God did not change after we ate the poisonous fruit.

   We perceived that God had changed...so we ran and hid.

   We have been hiding in shame and fear from our projected "God" ever since.

2. The second significant consequence was that they were no longer able to see themselves accurately. They quickly resorted to guilt and blame, rather than seeing themselves as participants in the Great Dance. The poisonous deception took root immediately within their souls and severely distorted their perceptions about themselves. They now identified themselves as separated from a holy God because of their sin—leaving them feeling fearful, shameful, and wholly unworthy. Once we lose sight of God for Who They truly are, we cannot see ourselves as we truly are.

When we see God, Who is our mirror, through distorted lenses, we can't see ourselves accurately either.

CHAPTER 6: INFESTATION – SOMETHING SINISTER THIS WAY SLITHERS

Sin always, in every instance, has its consequences. This is designed into the equation from the onset. Deception leads to sin, which contains built-in reverberations, ultimately leading to destruction, disharmony, and pain. We shouldn't blame God for frying us if we grab a downed power wire (electricity) or blame God for splattering us if we step off a 25-story building (gravity). There are physical laws associated with electricity and gravity that have direct consequences as we interact with them—and so it is with the law of sin and death.

We are punished BY our sins;
we're not punished by God FOR our sins.
God is the Pursuer, the Healer.

God's Holiness

The massive mistake we made after eating the fruit is thinking that our distorted perceptions allowed us to recognize God's *holiness for the first time accurately*. We also assigned so much weight to Adam that we changed our perception of every human being's core identity from that moment. Instead of seeing our true holy nature that bore the Divine imprint (and was declared "very good"), we saw a false evil sin nature that was permanent and irreversible. After this, we believed it required a perfect blood sacrifice to remove the massive separation gap between God and us. In one sweeping move, *we unknowingly became Universalists for the effects of Adam's sin!*

Can we see the massive logical flaw here? We believe that deception and sin provide us with our first accurate perception of the Creator's "holiness"!? We mistakenly assigned to God a character trait that we defined *after* sin entered into the picture, not realizing that our fear of this "holy God" was utterly unfounded. As we will see in a moment, God is the One Who pursues and covers His shame-ridden children. As time went on (especially during the Enlightenment Period), our understanding of "holiness" changed. It went from representing the set-apart, otherworldly, pure flow of shared intimate love within the pre-Creation Divine Sanctuary (which every person was designed to enjoy) to the sinless standard of perfection that no one could attain.

Meanwhile, this counterfeit "God-projection," a result of the deadly *PoisIF* in our soul-garden, would emphasize from this point forward, a perfect, holy God and our wretched sinful nature that so obviously separated us from Him. The *PoisIF* would continue to shape man's distorted views of the Divine and cause humanity to be severely seduced by a sinister cycle of sin and sickness as the Story slowly unfolded. This distorted image became our default identity—*dirty, worthless sinners separated from a holy God.*

Relentless Pursuit

Stay with this a moment longer. I missed this interaction for several decades, though I'd read it hundreds of times. Can you picture this scene, really get a vivid image of the tenderness here? It is not the furious judge pounding his gavel and saying in disgust, "Away with you!!" It's the Three-in-Love coming toward Adam and Eve, purposefully designing clothes from animal skins, and tenderly helping them get dressed as a means of addressing their shame and guilt. God's "fury" toward the deception and sin, flowing from an intense love for Their children, motivated a response to invite them out of the deceit and back into the truth of their union. See it?

> **Gen. 3:21 (MSG)** GOD made leather clothing (long coats or tunics of skins) for Adam and his wife and dressed them. GOD said, "The Man has become like one of us, capable of knowing everything, ranging from good to evil. What if he should reach out and take fruit from the Tree of Life and eat, and live forever? Never—this cannot happen!"

What an amazing act of God, a striking shadow of the Love demonstrated on the Cross!

Again, the key take-away from this scene is that God did not change after man's disobedience. We did! Man saw God through different lenses, now affected severely by the *PoisIF* of the false spirit...a god-projection formed from our deep sense of separation that produces inner fear, darkness, and confusion. We hide from this "god" in our minds, and from ourselves, behind the fig leaves. But still, God comes for us, before any thought we have about repenting. God is always reaching for us amid our deception... and always will.

CHAPTER 6: INFESTATION – SOMETHING SINISTER THIS WAY SLITHERS

Flaming Swords at the Entrance

Notice the ending of this scene at the east end of Eden's garden, when Adam and Eve are "banished," and angels are set in place to guard the entrance with flaming swords. This is a beautiful picture of God's invitation for them to return to the place of intimate connection! God would not have them return in the same state of alienation and perceived separation as when they left. To return to the garden, they would have to pass through the flaming sword.

The fire of God's love stands guard at the entrance to our soul-garden. Its purpose is to burn away all the lies and deceptions, fear and shame, and perceived separation that comes from our sin so that we might return to the awareness of the intimacy and union in Christ that we have been designed to enjoy. The gates are always open, the invitation always offered, but the flames are ever in place to remove the internal barriers that prevent us from receiving the full weight of Christ's love. This holy fire also has the power and nuance to penetrate the deepest, most hidden places within the soul—mind, and heart—and do its healing work smack dab in the depths of our darkness.

In summary, the Garden of Eden is also our soul-garden and features a God that continues to initiate, reveal Themselves, and invite us back into the original Paradise-like relationship within the Divine Sanctuary. God recognizes the overwhelming human urges within us for pleasure, identity, and purpose and asks us to look inward and drink freely from the Divine Flow as the only true Reality that will satisfy.

Black Hole Takeaway from the Great Deception

A deadly virus of deception infected humankind in the Garden, leading toward a false narrative that we are born dirty, worthless, and sinful—separated from a holy, righteous God. The truth is that separation from God *equals* non-existence because God is our very Source and the Sustenance of life itself. We must start the narrative in Genesis 1, *not* Genesis 3.

Chapter 7
Imitation – Rise of the Deepfake
(Genesis 4 - End of Malachi)

The *PoisIF* creates within our soul an incredibly powerful "vacuum" that wants to feed the part of itself that believes it is separated from God and from each other. The surrounding culture (the "mind of the world") waits in eager anticipation to rush into our soul and create a false sense of fulfillment, keeping us locked inside a fake existence.

INTO THE ABYSS

Interior Cravings

Deep inside each one of us is a
non-negotiable need for
value, significance,
belonging,
worth.

If we don't become aware of
the One Who created us,
the One Who longs
to be our Source
    of Life,

We become human suction devices
  powered by constant cravings deep within, attempting to suck life
    from everything around us, and we will even resort to violence
      in order to satisfy the cravings of our false selves.

We turn to money,
  pleasure,
    work,
      experiences,
        morality.

Without knowing it,
  we turn to other people
    trying to suck life
      from our relationships.

All of us were hand-crafted to look inward and
  draw our Identity and Meaning from Christ.

The Divine Flow satisfies the deepest cravings of our soul.
Don't rely on the counterfeit
  When the Genuine
    Wants to set your heart
      On Fire.

CHAPTER 7: IMITATION – RISE OF THE DEEPFAKE

A Whopping Lie in Junior High

In the early 2000s, I took a personal development class for work to increase self-awareness in our interactions with others based on our personality. In one of the exercises, we closed our eyes and imagined a scene from childhood that was significant in "shaping" us. The memory that surfaced caught me off guard.

I was back in junior high at Grace Baptist Academy in the exercise, and I was walking down the stairs heading to our next class. At the time, I was "going steady" with one of the prettiest girls in our class. I was extremely self-conscious socially at that age, especially around girls, so the height of this "relationship" involved sitting together at school events, passing secret notes in class, and exchanging shy smiles throughout the school day.

Anyway, as I turned a corner on my way to class, I found myself behind a group of guys from my class who didn't know I was there. They were laughing and horsing around as we often did, and someone brought up the girl I was "dating." One guy, a tall, athletic kid, turned and responded with something that affected me far deeper than I ever knew when it first happened. He was interested in the same girl, and he knew she was mine at the time.

He said jokingly, *"What in the world would ANY girl EVER see in Mo?!?"* He was only doing what teenage boys do—making his case why he was the right guy, and I could never be. And though now it seems so small and insignificant to assign such weight to this phrase spoken in passing, I did precisely that. My brain forgot it immediately, but apparently, my heart held on and buried it deep. This moment was, I believe, the *birth of my fake identity*.

In high school, college, and well into adulthood, I set out to do everything I could to prove my worth. I became class president, MVP of our basketball team, Illinois state scholar, valedictorian, church youth group leader, MVP of our college tennis team, winner of piano competitions, and recipient of an academic scholarship to the #2 engineering college in the nation at the time. If I did anything, I would excel—not to outperform anyone else, but because I was in a fierce battle within myself to prove my worth.

Little did I know then that I was skillfully creating a very convincing body-and-soul avatar from my intense shame and insecurity, based on a long-held lie that I wasn't enough—and would never be enough. To anyone on the outside, I was successful to the highest levels in so many areas, to the point where other parents pointed to me as an example for their kids. But inside, I was just a scared little boy with horrible self-esteem that wore "performance" and "people-pleasing" masks as his primary identity.

This wasn't a significant trauma or abuse like some have suffered in their lives, so I don't want to exaggerate. I don't think the kid in front of me in that hallway even knew I was listening! But for me, it was a "shaping event" that planted a lie deep into the soil of my soul and ended up driving my life—a false identity that steered me down a counterfeit story.

I began to realize a whole slew of other such statements and circumstances that reinforced this same mistaken identity, embedding themselves into my mind and heart in ways that remained well hidden from my awareness. While there are thousands of possible reactions to "shaping events"—words and deeds inflicted on us by people and circumstances beyond our control—the underlying and life-shaping lies of fear, shame, insecurity, and confusion are often the same.

This lie stayed concealed for over 20 years in my subconscious mind before it showed up in my awareness. Deception can be deadly and incredibly challenging to detect in ourselves, especially when the heart stores up painful memories of which the mind remains totally unaware. Over time, a steady progression of overwhelming and debilitating life events came at me to the point where I lost all control, as they radically impacted essential sources of my security—false identities, masks. As I described in the Prologue, my perceived identity took major beatings as life's earthquakes shook me to my core.

My soul-garden was so well-fertilized with the *PoisIF* that I didn't recognize what had been growing since junior high. My identity...was a complete counterfeit. I was about to meet...*my Deepfake*.

The Deepfake Identity

Early in 2020, while facilitating a course on deep learning, Alex Amini, a doctoral student at MIT, invited a special guest to introduce the topic: former president Barack Obama, who joined the class via videoconference. After a short welcome, he described the revolutionary aspects of deep learning and artificial intelligence coming to the forefront in modern

CHAPTER 7: IMITATION – RISE OF THE DEEPFAKE

science. At the end of the video, the class was shocked—Obama shared that the video they were watching at the time was not real. It was what we call now a "Deepfake."

A Deepfake is an artificial intelligence-based algorithm that uses deep neural networks to create a doctored video.[30] The face and body movements of an actor are translated to a target—in this case, President Obama. These videos can be incredibly convincing, and it's sometimes nearly impossible to distinguish a Deepfake from the real thing. In the last several years, this technology was used to remaster Princess Leia in *Star Wars: Rogue One*, insert Donald Trump into a *Breaking Bad* scene as a parody, have Facebook CEO Mark Zuckerburg deliver a fake address, and bring artist Salvador Dali back to life as a host at the museum in Florida that bears his name.

Though its usage so far has been mainly neutral, one can easily imagine the danger when in the wrong hands. A politician from Florida called this the modern equivalent of a nuclear weapon. Think about the effects of a realistic fake video with a seemingly legitimate threat to national security as one of a dozen examples. By the time it's identified as a fake, damage may have already been done. The Deepfake is a game-changer when it comes to technology.

I'm amazed at how closely this resembles the process of how our false self is created.

Our subconscious mind, infused with the *PoisIF*, uses its deep neural network to process the bits of information collected over a lifetime, and sends it through a complex internal algorithm. This mind machine then generates a persuasive Deepfake "avatar," a doctored projection of our subconscious mind, which naturally believes and acts as if it's the real thing. Our minds do what they are wired to do—they process all inputs and compile them into a perceived identity. We believe we are, in fact, our thoughts, feelings, beliefs, sensations, memories, abuses—and all the other inputs that have made up our lives.

To make it worse, since everyone has their own Deepfake, we reinforce each other's illusions so thoroughly and convincingly that most of us have no idea whatsoever that our "Real Identity" exists apart from all this. What a dastardly and powerful system we must contend with! This is the "world

---

30. Dickson, Ben. What is a Deepfake? https://www.pcmag.com/news/what-is-a-deepfake PCMag.com, March 4, 2020. Accessed June 9, 2020.

system" that the scriptures warn us about so often—the *"be not conformed to this world"* matrix where we live as Deepfake avatars in a world built primarily from our own perceptions. The *PoisIF* strain can take a million different forms, which I've broken into three broad categories.

Deadly Strains of the *PoisIF*

Category One	Category Two	Category Three
Wrong Choices or Difficult Circumstances	The Culturally Defined "Good Life"	The Religiously Defined "Good Life"
Drug addiction, alcoholism, gluttony, pornography, gambling, violence, materialism, trauma, abuse, neglect	Food, shopping, marriage and family, experiences, exercise, friends, entertainment, social media, work, plans for future	Studying scripture, praying, attending church, ministering, serving in community, going on mission trips, worshipping, fellowshipping, resisting sin

The examples in these categories—from porn to prayer, from crack cocaine to community service, from materialism to ministry—can easily become counterfeit sources of life and identity. The subtle, brutal deception is that all of these things, or *responses* to these things, can prevent us from seeing Truth. We don't find our real life from law-abiding or sin-avoiding, success-achieving, or pain-numbing. Every one of these becomes part of the algorithm in our subconscious that creates our Deepfake false self.

Inside the world system, most of us remain "practically" blind to the existence of the Real World (the Kingdom of God...the Divine Sanctuary), though we may intellectually acknowledge that it exists. Our Deepfake has an insatiable need for comfort, security, and certainty and rises to protect itself from any threat of transformational truth that might infiltrate the bubble of soul safety inside our illusion. The *PoisIF* within us goes rogue, masterfully designed to penetrate our deepest core and multiply into a full-fledged self-deception, keeping us locked within a mental prison of our own making.

As the poison makes its way through our system, our subconscious minds distract us with anything in the known universe to satisfy the infinite inner cravings within. They demand to be fed—the good, bad, ugly,

CHAPTER 7: IMITATION – RISE OF THE DEEPFAKE

inspirational, spiritual—anything that will keep our Deepfake alive and thriving and prevent us from experiencing our life and identity in Christ. We see and process the mirage and believe it as reality.

Love Your Enemies

Our hearts can store up an incredible library of memories that remain entirely hidden from our minds. This is what happened to me with the incident from junior high. It eventually led me to spend time in all three categories above, though I ended up establishing the central portion of my identity in the religious "ings" of Category Three. Why? Well, I had been taught and became convinced that God needed me to do these for Him to be pleased with me...or at least, less disappointed. I was proud of my false self, built on all the religious doings, and thought I was a pretty spiritually mature guy overall. I was mistaken. Unbeknownst to me at the time, my entire life was based on the *foundational lie of separation*.

All of these strains are symptoms of underlying issues, clues of the lies that are causing them. Rather than trying to demolish the symptoms or ignore them too quickly, it's worth asking what they're showing us about our core beliefs and our self-identity...why we're spending our time and energy on coping, numbing, distracting, pursuing, people-pleasing, and God-appeasing.

I'm still learning to do this. I had been taught to run at full speed away from any hint of "sinful" behaviors, or to run directly at them with a raised sword to destroy them. But when we're only looking to get rid of symptoms, we're only doing sin management or sin avoidance, which doesn't lead us toward wholeness. It's sort of like putting a piece of duct tape over the flashing "check engine light" on our car's instrument panel, thinking that we're solving our issue. As we all know, the flashing light is only an external indicator of a deeper internal problem. Our unhealthy behaviors are like this flashing light—a sign that we need to look "under the hood" and see what's going on.

I've found great value in befriending my inner shadow side, asking *why* I see certain symptoms, and then listening closely. Jesus' command to "love your enemies" doesn't only apply to other people. We also need to love the dark and challenging parts of ourselves, and turn our inner enemies into friends over time. *This* leads our souls toward wholeness.

Prov. 20:27 (NASB) The spirit of man is the lamp of the Lord, searching all the innermost parts of his being.

Warning: Our Deepfake identity is highly skeptical and suspicious of thoughtful, Spirit-led inner evaluation that might present evidence that it is a counterfeit. It feels threatened with the idea of a Real World or a True Self and will fight like a banshee to protect its existence. This will usually mean ignoring, criticizing, or numbing, so that it can continue living with its counterfeit sense of peace, insulation, and comfort. We must pay attention to the "flashing lights" in our lives!

Repent!

If we can pause long enough, we see that our soul lenses have been severely affected by our own shame, confusion, and insecurity. We have painted counterfeit images of God in our minds because of these demoralizing thoughts. Still, God is always confronting these distortions and revealing Truth in language that speaks to our souls. When we run from God in our shame and fear…when we ignore the issues, or continuously self-criticize, or numb our pain and loneliness in a thousand different ways…the One Who loves us runs toward us with hand-fashioned clothes to cover us. The Three-in-Love's burning desire is to heal these broken parts within us and restore our original identity.

> *Our greatest "sin" is believing in a distorted portrait of God's character.*

It helps to picture our intimidating inner pile of fear and darkness… and hear God whispering with otherworldly confidence…"Let's address the roots of these things together. I am the Great Physician and I have the remedy for this deadly poison—the lie that keeps you from living out your real life. Here…let me wrap your soul in the Truth. And don't fear the Flame—it is designed to burn away all that keeps you from fully receiving My love."

We find that this isn't the loud, condemning voice of the angry street preacher or the turn-or-burn evangelist behind the pulpit. Instead, this is the gentle, firm Voice of the One Who birthed us and wants to be intimately involved in our life. The more we get to know, and tangibly experience, the

CHAPTER 7: IMITATION – RISE OF THE DEEPFAKE

Spirit of Christ within, the more we learn to recognize this Voice, whose primary language is silence. To our great surprise, the Voice of God might "sound" a lot like our own voice. Can we trust this quiet Whisper within us?

This is the Voice above all other voices that we must tune our hearts and minds to listen for. Instead of separating Themselves from us because of our "sinfulness," They come toward us to persuade us of Their true nature (and ours), to show us the deep deceptions we don't even know we have—so they can be burned away. Once we behold the Truth of God, repentance (in the Greek, this is *metanoia* or μετάνοια – a change of mind) comes without effort.

REPENT (change your mind about God) and experience Christ as your Life.

We are not in the process of becoming someone or something else. We are discovering who, and whose, we truly are—asking God to help us experience what They already know is true in Reality.

Gold Dust: Abba's Sense of Humor

Many years after starting over from scratch with my faith journey, I was involved in a book study about the stages of a man's spiritual growth with a few other guys. One of the things I realized during our study was that I had always longed for a mentor, an older man who could teach and show me what it looked like to transition from boyhood to manhood. In many ways, I think this was because I was still a scared, insecure little kid trapped in an adult body.

I had several strong, influential mentors over the years: Pastor Sam, who made me feel like the most important person in the room when he saw me. He taught me the value of sitting in silence before God. Chaplain Stan, an older brother who carried a rough history, who served as a janitor where I worked. He had a broad smile and a huge heart, and he showed me that a small act of love was far more influential than articulating an accurate theology. Pastor Brent, who showed me that the supernatural should be natural as I began experiencing miraculous healings for the first time.

But despite these significant influences, which I remain grateful for, I realized eventually that my soul longed for my Dad to be my primary mentor. He was the one I had been performing for during my impressionable years, continually trying to gain his attention and approval. I will always be grateful for my parents' diligence, hard work, and incredible sacrifices for our family, accompanied by their simple faith. They shared all the knowledge they were aware of with me. I realized that I was trying to force something beyond what Dad could give, because his Dad hadn't mentored him in that way. It took a long time to release him from this expectation, but my longing was ever-present.

So, I asked God to be my Mentor...to be my Daddy. I wasn't sure what that really meant at the time or what to expect. During this period, I was also heavily involved in a few Charismatic groups. Miraculous healing, prophetic words, and supernatural signs and wonders burst onto my radar. These things were framed as "dangerous" while growing up in a conservative Baptist/Brethren environment, but I was eating up all this explosive Holy Spirit activity!

One Sunday evening, after a particularly fiery prayer gathering at a local church, I was walking out and overheard the pastor talking to someone about what had happened recently during a morning worship service. He said that gold dust started sprinkling inside the sanctuary during one of the songs. What?! Gold dust materializing out of nowhere? Where was this ever mentioned in the Bible, and what was the point? I had seen the stories of healing, prophecies, and miracles in the scriptures—but gold dust? Ha!! I laughed under my breath, scoffing as I walked out. I secretly wondered if they had planted some glitter in the rafters and then staged it to look like a miracle.

Several weeks later, I was at the bathroom sink, getting ready for work early in the morning. When I looked in the mirror, I saw a single speck of gold dust on my left cheek, just above my upper lip. My daughter, Delani, was around four years old at the time, so I figured it was probably glitter or something from one of her crafts. I brushed it off, not giving it a second thought as I finished getting ready for work.

A few days later, at the sink again early in the morning, I looked up and saw another single speck of gold dust in the same spot as last time. I stared at it for a few seconds, then laughed at the coincidence as I wiped it away and left for work.

Several days later, the same scene. This time when I saw it, in that EXACT same spot, I stared, wide-eyed. At that moment, it felt like God reached over and tenderly touched my cheek with His index finger. From

CHAPTER 7: IMITATION – RISE OF THE DEEPFAKE

my deep spirit, I heard these words: "My child, I heard your prayer, and I will be your Daddy...your Mentor." I put my face in my hands, and wept like a baby for several minutes, overcome with shock and emotion. God had responded to me, right in the middle of my skepticism. What an incredibly intimate memory... and what a sense of humor They have!!

After that incident, I continued to see a single gold speck in that same spot on my cheek infrequently but regularly. It melted my soul every time. On several occasions, when I was at a low point, I would look in a mirror and see one, and a rush of warm assurance would flood over me. As I've been writing this book, I've seen a few more.

Just as an additional "wink" from God, every so often, I would see a single speck of gold in some random place, always causing me to smile—on the couch, in my car, on someone's face, on my clothes—but mostly, on my own cheek.

For me, these are tender moments of Divine affection and affirmation, stretching all the way back to deconstruct that whopping lie from junior high. The Voice above all other voices was whispering that I am enough, that I am Their delight, that others' words and expectations say something about *them* and *not* about me. It took me some time, but eventually, I became fully persuaded of God as my tender Abba (AND my nurturing Mama), Who loves me the same way Jesus was loved. My soul was finally able to rest as I saw God for who They were, and I repented for the lies I had embraced about myself.

INTO THE ABYSS

REFLECTION...What lies have I believed about who I am? God, help me see how my mind has filtered my history to make me believe things about myself that aren't the truth because this isn't the way You see me. I call out the lies I know about for what they are—counterfeits, distortions, imprisonment. I trust that lies I'm not yet aware of will come to the surface as well—not to dwell on and regurgitate—but to be exposed as frauds. Some lies have affected me deeply, and I trust that they will burn away in the holy heat of Christ's love.

> **Black Hole Takeaways from the Deepfake Identity**
>
> - The Deepfake identity is a self-deception powered by influences in the body and soul, which mainly dwell in our subconscious mind.
>
> - The most effective cure for our false identity is a tangible encounter with the Truth of Christ.

After Genesis 3, the remainder of the Old Testament is a series of sharp roller-coaster twists and turns, loopty-loops and bendy bends, unusual ups and dizzying downs, displaying the dastardly effects of the *PoisIF* on every aspect of human life. But amidst all of it is the God who relentlessly pursues us to re-reveal Truth in our hearts.

What we really needed all along was a Genesis 1-2 reminder of who we were, a mirror of who we had been created to be. It took some time, but we were given the gift of our mirror. Humanity, for the first time, saw its original design. God threw back the curtains and stepped onto the center stage. It was an extraordinary entry, but one that is helping us recover our True Selves.

PART II
Awakening the True Self

Questioning our beliefs is a great starting point . . .The rabbit hole deepens when we start questioning reality itself.

"Be who you were created to be, and you will set the world on fire."
St. Catherine of Sienna
Mystic, Activist, Author, Doctor of the Church

"The atoms or elementary particles themselves are not real; they form a world of potentialities or possibilities rather than one of things or facts."
Werner Heisenberg
German Theoretical Physicist, Pioneer of Quantum Mechanics

Chapter 8
Incarnation – Arrival of Our True Mirror
(Matthew - John)

Jesus came to show us the true nature of God, His Abba. He does this by coming and looking out from *inside* our self-imposed darkness, fear, and shame...and then telling us the Truth. In doing this, He showed us *our* true nature and our Divine Origin that we had so severely forgotten. He came as humanity's true mirror, a flashback to the God-breathed nature deposited into us by the Spirit.

Cure for the *PoisIF*

As we jump several thousand years forward in the Story, in an unlikely stable in Bethlehem, we see the arrival of a strange cure. God comes to earth, not because of any need or lack, but because They chose to enter our darkness. They came as the self-sacrificial expression of Trinitarian love to remind man of our place within the Divine Fellowship. Rather than sending a magic potion filled with a supernatural elixir for the *PoisIF*, God came and took on our flesh so that They might provide us a most unusual form of the cure—a form that subverted the expectation of everyone waiting for its arrival.

> *The solution for the PoisIF came as a zygote in the womb of an unwed peasant girl.*

INTO THE ABYSS

> **Luke 2:19 (VOICE)** Mary, too, pondered all of these events, treasuring each memory in her heart.

If there's any "sin" that Jesus came to save us from, it was the deadly *PoisIF* lie of "separation from a holy God because of our sin," which distorted our portraits of God so horrifically back in Eden's garden. For thousands of years, those who faithfully studied their scriptures formed very confident assertions about what God was like. They got it completely and utterly wrong when God actually came to us in the flesh. But they were so confident of their scripturally backed god-portraits, that they eventually killed the real God to defend their counterfeit perceptions of God.

Jesus is the Truth about God, spoken in Love.

God was never holding our sins against us. Love doesn't keep a record of wrongs, and Their desire is to heal us of anything that keeps us from experiencing the full weight of Their love and delight toward us. We needed to know this once and for all. God was in Christ, reconciling the whole world to Himself, not counting men's sins against them.

> **2 Cor. 5: 19a (VOICE)** It is central to our good news that God was in the Anointed making things right between Himself and the world. This means He does not hold their sins against them...

The Cosmic Christ

Is there any distinction between the historical human we know as Jesus of Nazareth and the eternal, universal Spirit that is the Christ we encountered in the pre-Beginning? Isn't "Christ" just Jesus' last name?

Yes, there's a difference. It's a nuanced distinction, though, so I don't want to get hung up on semantics because both are fully and personally present in Jesus Christ. But Christ didn't exist *in human form* until incarnated in the person of Jesus.

The main distinction I see is that the revelation of the Cosmic Christ— the One in whom the entire Creation was formed, sustained, and held together—manifests organically and beautifully in people around the globe. Folks in such varied circumstances and locations, many of whom

CHAPTER 8: INCARNATION – ARRIVAL OF OUR TRUE MIRROR

have never known or heard the name "Jesus," live their lives based on a foundation of love. This is the essential, transcendent nature of God manifesting in all places, as people respond to the light they've been given by living and acting from their True Self, hidden with God in Christ.

There seems to be a universal awareness that God (Love) is the highest ideal, a sign that this has been hard-wired into our DNA. This transcendent, universal nature serves as a beautiful complement to God's intimate, personal nature that we see in the incarnation of God in Jesus. I believe we need both the transcendent aspect of God in Christ and the personal aspect of God we find in Jesus.

This is profound and significant to me: We see the infinite expressions of Christ in Jesus (content and character) who embodied the Spirit in human form for some 33 years. But before, during, and after Jesus was here, the Spirit of Christ sustains and holds together the entire universe. Jesus said it would be *better* for us that He go away, perhaps because He knew the limitations of believing that God is only accessible in certain places or people (see John 16:7).

In my experience, the language around the human "Jesus" is often more exclusive than we realize. It can minimize the reality that the Spirit of Christ exists eternally outside of time, a universal Presence that is continuously and creatively revealing our Divine Origin.

So, Jesus came to reveal the eternal and unshakeable Reality, the Truth of our original identity in Christ—the source and substance of which the Spirit of Christ continually bears universal witness. And when we learn to see Jesus after the Spirit, and not after the flesh, we can begin entering this Reality that He came to reveal.

> **2 Cor. 5:16 (AMPC)** Consequently, from now on we estimate *and* regard no one from a [purely] human point of view [in terms of natural standards of value]. [No] even though we once did estimate Christ from a human viewpoint *and* as a man, yet now [we have such knowledge of Him that] we know Him no longer [in terms of the flesh].

INTO THE ABYSS

Boundaries

I don't want to stray
  But I know I can't stay
    Within the walls of
      Theological structures
       That attempt to
         Constrain Reality.

I was taught
  The God of Christians…
    But now I dream
      About Christ
       Of the entire
         Cosmos.

Jesus is God…We are "gods"

When we experience Jesus as the mirror aspect of God, we see our fully human selves as "gods" (little g). If we can grasp this, we might stop judging the experience of our humanness as being wrong or unholy or separated from God because we're in a body. The passage below explains the connection Jesus is making between the human and the divine as He responds to the religious leaders:

> **John 10:33-36 (VOICE)**
>
> **Jews:** You are not condemned for performing miracles. We demand Your life because You are a man, yet you claim to be God. This is blasphemy!
>
> **Jesus:** You know what is written in the Scriptures. Doesn't it read, "I said, you are gods"? If the Scriptures called your ancestors (mere mortals) gods to whom the word of God came—and the Scriptures cannot be set aside—what should you call One who is unique, sanctified by and sent from the Father into the world? I have said, "I am God's Son." How can you call that blasphemy?

CHAPTER 8: INCARNATION – ARRIVAL OF OUR TRUE MIRROR

Jesus is saying here, paraphrased, "Everyone in a body, regardless of the degree of awareness or the morality of their actions, are gods—because all have been created in the image of the Divine. Yes, even those who are thoroughly confused about their own identity. Even the overtly religious folks, those who condemn, judge, and kill the innocent, all are gods...as are the whores, the cheats, the unclean, the non-religious. It makes no difference. If you show up in a seemingly polluted, separated state of being, you are still gods."

> *"God became man so that man would become God."*
> **St. Athanasius**[31]

Then we have part two of his statement, again paraphrased, "Then how much more am I a God? I am "sanctified" by the Spirit so I can operate with a higher awareness of my Union with our Abba. I can maintain constant conscious contact with and be fully animated by God's love for me and my love for Them. How can you say I am not God?"

The essence of Jesus' story is that all are "gods." We are all partakers of the Divine, all branches on the Christ-Vine. So, instead of judging other humans as fallen and needing to seek holiness, we should accept our intrinsic holiness gifted to us before the worlds were formed and then start to love ourselves as God does. This is the narrow gate to life that many have yet to find. By loving ourselves, seeing the Divine spark in all, and loving them as God has loved us...this is the way we demonstrate our love for the Divine.

> **1 John 4:7 (NASB)** Beloved, let us love one another, for love is from God; and everyone who loves is born of God and knows God.

A More Childlike God

Jesus, our true mirror sent from God, was the most "childlike" adult in history. He was an innocent One Who grew through all of the stages of human existence, yet retained all that we recognize as beautiful in children. He matured physically, mentally, spiritually, and socially without letting responsibility, culture, stereotypes, expectations, or perceptions

---

31. Athanasius, "Section 54", *On the Incarnation*, De inc. 54, 3: PG 25, 192B, Independent Publishing Platform, April 20, 2017.

ever change His original state of innocence. Nothing kept Him from being fully aware, fully present, fully Himself, in every situation. "Unless you become like little children," He said, "you cannot see or enter the Kingdom of God." He knew that the God of Creation was His tender Abba, and in that tender Union He lived His human life. The following are just some of His magnificent characteristics:

Radical Trust	Able to rest wholly and completely in the intimate Union He shared with His Abba
Relentless Curiosity	Sustained awe/delight in circumstances and people and Creation; filled with possibility
Rich Relationships	No judgmental labels on people; interacted with them according to their True Identity
Ridiculous Freedom	Able to fully, confidently express Himself in any situation without care of what others perceived or expected; not bound to existing rules of time management or societal norms

This man was the True Human, holding up a mirror for us to see our true lives, hidden with God in Christ. We are animated by the same Spirit and loved unconditionally by the same Abba.

> **Col. 3:3 (AMPC)** For [as far as this world is concerned] you have died, and your [new, real] life is hidden with Christ in God.

> **Ps. 139:13-15 (AMPC)** For You did form my inward parts; You did knit me together in my mother's womb. I will confess and praise You for You are fearful and wonderful and for the awful wonder of my birth! Wonderful are Your works, and that my inner self knows right well. My frame was not hidden from You when I was being formed in secret [and] intricately and curiously wrought [as if embroidered with various colors] in the depths of the earth [a region of darkness and mystery].

My *real* life is hidden with Christ in God, Who hand-crafted me for Themselves, identified with me so that I can identify myself completely and fully in Them. I no longer need to seek "life" from any other source. In Jesus Christ, the One Who fully expresses the Godhead...the cosmos, and all of humankind find their source and harmony (see John 1:1-9).

CHAPTER 8: INCARNATION – ARRIVAL OF OUR TRUE MIRROR

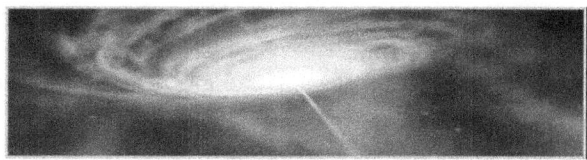

Mirrors and Shop Windows: The Kurzweil 250

During my high school and college years, I was heavily influenced by the wide range of popular synth-bands that defined the music of the '80s. As a result, I went gaga over synthesizers. I immersed myself in reading about the latest and greatest and finally started shopping to get one for myself. My dream was the Kurzweil 250, a beautiful piece of keyboard technology that could replicate a $50,000 concert grand piano. It had built-in effects and thousands of sounds, along with a sequencer and several other features that reduced me to a drooling baby in a high chair as I would read the ads.

On many occasions, I would go into a local music store and sample the keyboards. I remember the first time I got to play a Kurzweil. What a thrill! Of course, it was so ridiculously out of my price range that I never remotely considered it a real possibility ever to own one. I settled for a Korg Poly-800 as my first keyboard for a few hundred dollars, then later upgraded to a used Korg M1 for about $1200. The best I could do was read the ads, stop by the store on occasion, and drool over the beauty I could never have.

Dear brothers and sisters, take this deep into your hearts...Because of Christ, we aren't "window shopping" when it comes to the things of God—things that at one point seemed so far out of our grasp. We look at Jesus' record—His spectacular miracles, courageous confrontation of influential leaders, unwavering trust in His Abba—and we place Him on such a high pedestal that we feel obligated to worship Him. Yet, we rarely feel compelled to follow His ways. We believe the gap between Jesus and us is far too significant to see Him as an example, other than admiring Him from afar, heads bowed and eyes closed.

No! We miss Jesus' message to us altogether when we limit ourselves to seeing Him this way. In Jesus, we are *gazing into a mirror*, seeing what is already true within us! We can't delight in God, worship Them, or express our love to Them unless we *first know* that They are eternally delighted with us, "worship" (assign an infinitely high value to) us, and express Their love to us—even before Creation. What a joy to discover that the Scriptures aren't a list of unattainable qualities we need to feverishly strive toward until we die. Instead, they are a treasure chest filled with unlimited riches that the God of the galaxies has deposited in us by Their Spirit.

Do we believe Jesus when He said that we'd do greater works than He did? What is God's by nature is given to us by the gift of Their glorious grace.

> **1 John 4:17b (NASB)** "... as He is, so also are we in this world."

I used to think these "greater works" were mostly about performing spectacular miracles, but it's so much deeper than that. I believe it's ultimately the gift of union with God, made available to us in Christ before the foundation of the world, as a means of sharing freely in Their Divine life (Eph. 1:4). Jesus shows us how to live in this present world as a representative of another realm, the one we encountered in the pre-Creation, filled with otherworldly possibilities. And unless we become like little children, there's a high chance that we'll miss it altogether.

Lost Coins and Lost Images

We see other people...not as THEY are...but as WE are.

In response to the accusation that He was keeping company with "notorious sinners," Jesus told three parables in Luke 15 to throw back the veil and show us His heartfelt motivation. He describes a lost sheep, then a lost coin, and finally the lost (prodigal) son. Imagine the shock in the audience as Jesus described God as a lowly shepherd, a poor peasant woman, and an old man running through the street—irreverent and scandalous descriptions, conjuring up unclean, low-class images in that culture. This was a stark contrast to the God they knew—the One Who was altogether transcendent, "holy," and couldn't look upon sin.

Also, note that the lost sheep, coin, and son *first* belonged to the shepherd, woman, and father. His framework in responding to questions about sinners and outcasts was that something must first belong, in order to be lost. Don't think for a second that this was easy—listening for the religious leaders, who were standing there gnashing their teeth. They were shocked and furious, as they often were, at the words and ways of the Christ.

CHAPTER 8: INCARNATION – ARRIVAL OF OUR TRUE MIRROR

To be "lost" implies original belonging.

Let's look closer at the lost coin parable:

> **Luke 15:8-10 (VOICE)** "Or imagine a woman who has ten coins and loses one. Won't she light a lamp and scour the house, looking in every nook and cranny until she finds it? And when she finds it you can be sure she'll call her friends and neighbors: 'Celebrate with me! I found my lost coin!' Count on it—that's the kind of party God's angels throw every time one lost soul turns to God."

The coin's original value isn't affected in the slightest by the dirt, grime, stench (and yes, "sinful" behavior) that covers it. The widow in her little hut searches the dirt floor diligently until she finds her lost coin, then throws a party. Can we see God's heart in this story by His response to the accusation of hanging around "notorious sinners"? The only thing that the religious leaders could see was the dirt, grime, stench, and sins—much like religion today as it quickly, scornfully judges external appearances and behaviors. However, our beautiful God knows the original value of the original coin (something determined during pre-Creation) and searches in the dirt until They find it...until They find us and remind us of our original value.

As I heard so often growing up, Adam's fall permanently changed man's nature from good to evil the moment he and Eve disobeyed. This fatal act had the universal effect of seemingly infusing sin into the entire human race and setting up the concept of a "sin nature" as our default condition. Yet, we so tragically miss that man's original image was *never* destroyed; it was only covered and distorted by lies. This is what Jesus exposes throughout His entire ministry. He reminds us that God never saw us in the horrific way that much of religion has taught us. Our nature has always been "very good," but we have lost sight of this from the confines of our blindness and confusion.

A few chapters later, we see a follow-up example involving another coin:

> **Luke 20:21-25 (VOICE)** "Teacher," they said, "we know that you speak and teach what is right and are not influenced by what others think. You teach the way of God truthfully. Now tell us—is it right for us to pay taxes to Caesar or not?" He saw through their trickery and said, "Show me a Roman coin.

Whose picture and title are stamped on it?" "Caesar's," they replied. "Well then," he said, "give to Caesar what belongs to Caesar, **and give to God what belongs to God.**"

This isn't a simple encouragement to pay taxes without complaining. It was a violent, verbal, punch-in-the-mouth denial of a vast national political assumption when Caesar was considered the "Lord and Savior" of the people. Jesus is saying that the coins may display Caesar's image on them, but humans are stamped *with the image of their Creator*. We may have to render unto Caesar what is stamped with Caesar's image—the coin; however, we are to give to God what is stamped with God's image—*our whole life*. The declaration was stunning and scandalous as understood by those in the audience. Caesar was not Lord...Jesus was Lord!

Remember back to the eternal prequel of pre-Creation? That's where each person received their original value, assigned by God. Many don't know this reality of their original value, as there is much dirt, grime, stench, and sin that keeps us from seeing clearly (resulting from the *PoisIF*). But once we recognize this value in ourselves—once we see how God views us—then it becomes our joy and a great honor to share this reality with other "lost coins" in our spheres of influence. We get to show them their true Christ-identity so they may give their lives joyfully to the One Who stamped His image on their hearts.

We may be lost coins, but we have ALWAYS belonged to God. The Owner knows our original pre-Genesis identity and searches for us until we believe it.

When it comes to value, a crusty old coin purchased at a garage sale for a nickel may turn out to be worth a fortune if assessed by a professional coin collector familiar with its origin. This collector may offer $100,000 for this coin if they believe it is an extremely rare find. In this case, the value of the coin is determined by *both* the image stamped on it *and* the value assigned by one who is very familiar with coins.

Do you see this? The Source of the Universe sent us Their most prized possession—the beloved eternal Son in human form—to show us the lengths They were willing to travel out of love and desire. Our value is assessed by Their eternal image stamped on our heart, the Spirit-breath-print animating

CHAPTER 8: INCARNATION – ARRIVAL OF OUR TRUE MIRROR

our unique existence, and the infinite worth They assigned to each of us. Their desire to pursue our freedom and participation in the Great Dance flows from the incredible value They see in us. What a contrast to the *PoisIF* lie of our shameful unworthiness before a can't-look-at-sin god.

> *In Their eyes, **we** are of infinite worth.*

A Controversial Message

See why they so desperately wanted to kill the rebel carpenter rabbi from Nazareth? He confronted a harsh religious system, which in and of itself, was the result of the *PoisIF's* drastic effects. This system used a strategic set of "holiness codes" and "external criteria" to control and manipulate people, keeping them from experiencing their God-given freedom and original value. The leaders of the system wanted to maintain their hierarchy and sense of religious power, reminding people of their sinful separateness before a holy and just God. Jesus, on the other hand, wanted all of humanity to experience abundant life within the Divine Sanctuary of love that birthed us.

His methods were not your average nice guy, soft-spoken sales pitches as He made His way through the earth. Rather, the world witnessed an unrestrained hurricane raging along a precarious, unpredictable path of Love and Healing and Freedom and Glory that threatened to uproot and destroy the roots of the religious *us-vs-them* structures of the first century.

Jesus still wreaks the same havoc in our religious systems today.

> **2 Cor. 5:21** (AMPC) For our sake He made Christ [virtually] to be sin Who knew no sin, so that in *and* through Him we might become [endued with, viewed as being in, and examples of] the righteousness of God [what we ought to be, approved and acceptable and in right relationship with Him, by His goodness]...

REFLECTION...Abba, You gave us Your eternal Son as a mirror to help us recover our true identity. Look me straight in the eyes and tell me who I am. Don't let me look away or dismiss you or pretend I already know.

INTO THE ABYSS

No matter how alienated or unworthy I might feel, I know that this doesn't change the reality of Your union with me. Hold my gaze until my soul is fully and permanently persuaded of what's true.

Fires and Hobo Pies: A Father/Son Story

I don't know if this story quite fits into this section of the book. However, I LOVE it so very much; please forgive the lack of continuity as I share this treasured moment from many years ago. It's one of my all-time favorites . . .

When my son Daniel was about ten years old, he and I were planning to spend a weekend together at home while the girls were out of town. Our plans were modest; one of the most anticipated events was cooking up some hobo pies (sandwiches made in cast-iron skillets) over a backyard campfire and watching late-night movies under "blanket tents" in the family room. That whole week we were looking forward to hanging out, and I saw the anticipation building in his eyes as the weekend approached.

Simple plans, safe expectations, quality father-son time.

On Saturday evening, we went back to our fire pit and started gathering wood and kindling. I'm a bit of a pyromaniac at heart, so with a bonfire vision dancing in my eyes, we crafted a beautifully ventilated tee-pee structure that would cook up those hobo pies in no time flat. We stepped back to survey our work, and satisfied that this was the stuff of legends, I struck a match and dropped it in the center of our pile. The first raindrop fell. I looked up, not realizing the storm clouds that had gathered overhead. The drizzle began before I had a chance to get our fire started. It was genuinely childish, but inside me, I began to feel a wild disappointment beginning to swell.

After a few minutes of failed attempts, accompanied by the sound of thunder, I was quickly planning alternatives to salvage the evening and sell it to my son in a way that sounded equally exciting. At that moment, I had the distinct impression to ask Danny to pray for the fire. Rational thought immediately took over, and I dismissed it as wishful thinking...but the thought sharpened and poked me again instead of floating away. Again, I resisted as the drizzle turned into a steady rain. As I got up to leave, the words burst from my lips somehow—the request for him to pray for the

CHAPTER 8: INCARNATION – ARRIVAL OF OUR TRUE MIRROR

fire. He gave me a confused look, glanced up at the sky, then down at the fire, and back to me. He bowed his head and prayed a simple prayer for God to let us have a fire for our hobo pies.

My heart raced as I opened my eyes and stared at the pit, expectation building. After all, I had obeyed a "prompt" in line with the Father's heart, to let Daniel experience (rather than simply understand) the power of God, and also the simple act of sharing a special memory between father and son. I looked down at him, my heart now bursting full of faith, and lit the next match beside the wood. Nothing. A few more attempts, my heart still faith-filled, but perhaps a slight sliver of doubt now. Nothing. One by one, I emptied the matchbook, and now accompanying the disappointment, I recognized a hint of anger. It was one thing to offer up a "practice" attempt for my sake, but a cruel taunt in front of my impressionable son. Unacceptable. Inexcusable. And completely unnecessary.

The walk back to the house was embarrassingly painful and difficult for me. It was now close to a downpour, and my mind was hammering with justification and disappointment, crafting a reasonable explanation to put this thing in context for Daniel to understand. Granted, I'm sure he was just as happy to throw the hobo pies in the oven. No big deal. Probably no need to offer much of an excuse at all. It was raining—we'll do it another time. But here's the thing—it would have been fine had I not asked him to pray. That was the issue. As immature as it sounds, I was truly disappointed at that moment.

So, with an overly heavy heart, I asked him to start getting the blankets ready for a tent as I flipped on the oven. As I walked back to the table to grab the cast-iron skillets, I glanced out through the rain at our fire pit, my failed mini altar reminiscent of the dancing, bloody Baal prophets from the Elijah story in the Jewish scriptures.

A Raging Fire!

I stared dumbfounded. I blinked and shook my head, turned away, and looked back. Seriously. A fully formed fire, right there in the middle of that pit! It was a downpour by now, and the thing hadn›t even had a chance to get started. And yet, the bonfire I had pictured now danced before me, manifested and forever burned into my memory. With joy unspeakable in my heart, I called Danny over to the window, scared that it would disappear if I turned my head.

He stared, looked up at me with confusion, and then back out at the fire pit as a faint smile crossed his young face. That's the other picture burned into me. I raced into the downpour and cooked up the hobo pies over this glorious fire, and shouted silent praise to God, this One Who saw my immaturity and exaggerated disappointment, before stepping in and reminding me not to shape my theology on anything less than Who They are.

I don't know how much impact that kind of thing makes in a kid, maybe just one of those cool, random things that happen every once in a while. But for me, it was the simple love and *unlimited possibility* of God supplying fire in the rain for our hobo pies. Something shifted and clicked into place deep inside me that day, an experience in God that seared me forever. It was as profound as being healed from cancer and far more influential than the dangerous layers of doctrinal understanding stored in my brain over many years steeped in a lifeless religion. It helped me to identify one way that the **PoisIF** had effectively inoculated me against certain ways of the Spirit.

Somehow, years later, in situations where I'm screaming at God for not coming through for me, this memory has always brought a sense of stability to my heart. God is *not* the magic genie that gives us whatever we ask if we press all the correct theology buttons. Instead, They are fully present with us in the middle of every situation. Our Abba planted a seed of trust and the *power of POSSIBILITY* in both Danny and me that day.

With examples like this, along with many others, my confidence in Abba's tender Presence accelerated rapidly. It gained a solid foundation that has shifted my perspective of God from an abstract concept to a tangible reality. A billion times more than my hopes and desires for my kids, this heavenly Daddy was and is involved in the seemingly insignificant details of our world. With an entire universe to uphold, the Creator served up an insane-in-the-rain fire so I could cook up hobo pies for my son.

What an amazing memory of God as Daddy. What a memory with my son. Abba, teach me to trust You more. *Show us what's possible* when we see Jesus as our true mirror and Christ as our true life.

> ### Black Hole Takeaway from Incarnation
>
> Jesus came to us as our mirror—not as an unattainable example of perfection that demands our worship from a reverent distance, but as the True Human, our elder brother. He showed us what's possible when living in union with Abba, animated by Their Spirit.

Chapter 9
Implication – Christ-Expression in the World
(Acts - Jude)

Everything we do flows from the perception of our identity—every decision we will face and every experience we will have. Our *actual* identity is eternally established and cannot change. It's a given. However, our *perceived* identity will drive our existence. Do we identify with our spirit, which is Christ...or with our body and soul "Deepfake" avatar, which conjures up the convincing illusion of our false self, operating as a human being that is fundamentally separate from God and our world? This convincing illusion is what keeps most religions thriving today, unfortunately.

The Who and the Do

God's will is for us to be extensions of the Divine Flow here on earth so that those we meet might see us as Christ-mirrors, and discover the truth of their own identity. This goes for **whomever** we're with or **whatever** the environment or **wherever** the situation in which we find ourselves.

So...what if God doesn't notice any spiritual difference between a church pastor and a restaurant owner? Most in religious circles would see these as different because one is clearly "sacred ministry" while the other is just a "secular job" to earn a living...*right?* Well, God's ways aren't like ours, and Jesus certainly didn't choose the "ministerial" elite as His disciples, whom He believed would change the world. Look at His parables and interactions, and notice how many of the "heroes" in the scriptures were church leaders as we might think of them today.

INTO THE ABYSS

What if the only difference between a missionary in Madrid, an engineer in Ethiopia, a teacher in Tokyo, a nurse in Nepal, and a stay-at-home dad in Denmark is their sphere of influence? Their one-of-a-kind gift mix and their unique Spirit-breath-print identifying who they are in Christ?

We are all commissioned by God to be full-time, lifetime expressions of Their beauty and grace.

That's each and every one of us. It was a massive threat to the religious system when Jesus started communicating the ways of His Kingdom in first-century Palestine. He chose the least likely candidates (foreigners, enemies, outcasts, and sinners) to play the greatest roles in the stories He told and be the recipients of His greatest affections in the interactions He had. It got Him killed, eventually! One thing is for sure: this certainly requires us to adopt a different perspective when it comes to finding our purpose in life.

I often heard while growing up that we need to prioritize God above everything else. Jesus first, others second, you last (the J.O.Y. acronym). But once I finally discovered that God had prioritized *me* above everything else, I realized They want to be integrated into every aspect of my life and not just be one good thing, among many other things. They wanted to *BE* my life, which means I needed to let go of any other identity propping up my false self. There has never been any separation between secular and sacred, or between God and man, because everything in our lives and in the cosmos is being held together in Christ.

> **Eph. 2:10 (VOICE)** For we are the product of His hand, heaven's poetry etched on lives, created in the Anointed, Jesus, to accomplish the good works God arranged long ago.

The Integrated Life

I grew up as a basketball fanatic. During summers, my friends and I would play games into the hundreds, often ending in late nights under the lights. In the dead of winter, I'd shovel a section of driveway, put on some gloves, and shoot hoops for hours by myself. Later, when I started coaching varsity ball, I would spend hours diagramming plays, thinking through skills drills, watching college and NBA games, tracking stats, and evaluating matchups. I loved the game! One day, I heard a passionate Sunday sermon

CHAPTER 9: IMPLICATION – CHRIST-EXPRESSION IN THE WORLD

about giving more of my time to the Lord. I started feeling guilty about the time and energy I devoted to a secular activity like basketball—rather than sacred things like studying Scripture or prayer and fasting. I started cutting back on my hoop time and started increasing my spiritual disciplines instead. And with that, my passion dropped like a duck meeting a hunter's crosshairs.

Like it was yesterday, I still remember the whisper from God several months later when They laid a doozy on me: "Mo, what if We told you that We love the game of basketball more than you do?" It floored me. And it was one of the many doors I had to walk through on my way toward freedom. I wasn't leaving God at home when I played or coached.

The Divine Flow was present everywhere, and this reality helped me see that God was expressing Themselves through me all the time, not just during the "spiritual" parts of my existence. This same reframe happened with my love for books, movies, alternative and progressive hard rock music, gathering with friends around a good meal, and especially when I dove deep into the world of astronomy.

All of life is sacred when we are aware that God is here and near. The things that light our hearts on fire are likely hinting at what God has deposited into us by Their breath—areas where They'd like to express Their life through us.

Why wouldn't the risen Christ in and through us pioneer the most advanced technology; dream the most beautiful and breathtaking screenplays; compose the world's most compelling, heart-stirring music, and discover cures for the deadliest diseases? After all, the Spirit is intimately familiar with the inner workings of next-generation holographic smartphones operated by brain waves, the teleportation technology needed for advanced modes of transportation, the flow behind advanced environmental models built to bring about long-term stewardship of our planet, and the creative spark inspiring the most beautiful artistic expressions and explosions of generosity and self-sustaining global communities. God should be on display, and is, in all these areas…if we would only realize it. I believe They want us to dream ridiculous God-dreams in every sphere of our lives.

When our personal life vision starts aligning with God's vision for Their Creation, dangerous and delightful things become possible. *Everything is sacred*, everything exists in the atmosphere of the Divine, and everything has the potential to move the Story toward its glorious conclusion.

Go to Church or Be the Church

Church buildings worldwide are filled with business owners, parents, nurses, lawyers, bankers, clerks, mechanics, waiters, and artists who have never remotely considered that God has given them unique realms of real and difference-making influence. Church leaders would drastically expand God's Kingdom scope of operation (which requires a relinquishing of control) if they were able to recognize the outside-of-church "footprint" of those in their care.

Suppose leaders come alongside and serve their congregations to help each person first discover their true identity, then their specific spheres of influence. In that case, they can begin equipping them to recognize and exercise that influence. We'd be making a massive step in the right direction. 95% of church members have never considered the possibility that they have essential roles to play in the Story, and that they have a "calling" to that role—which is very likely located outside of the local church building, in what they consider a "secular" setting.

Many (like me) learned that the most significant impact they could make is giving money and time regularly to the church and other religious organizations because *they* were the ones with the real influence. We were told that our primary goal is to invite people to church so that the "professionals" can handle it. We need to be humble in this area. God looks for those who recognize when the Spirit is moving in ways different than our traditional mindsets may have allowed in past seasons and calls out those who are willing to follow the way of Jesus, often into uncharted territory.

> *We are all commissioned directly by God to be full-time, lifetime expressions of Love.*

God: Wholly "Other," Wholly "Same"

God is Love. When we hear this phrase, our first instinct might be to picture an example of human love that we've seen, heard about, or experienced ourselves, then multiply it by some gigantic factor and assign that mental "value" to God. Consider the entire planet full of people and allow your mind to extract all of the magnificent examples of love that have ever occurred. Now extend backward and forward through time to include every person that's ever lived and every person that ever will. Imagine that

CHAPTER 9: IMPLICATION – CHRIST-EXPRESSION IN THE WORLD

somehow we're able to morph all of these examples and pictures into a single act of love, such that it represents the most heart-wrenching, soul-engulfing, awe-inspiring scene that could ever occur or even be imagined.

> *God's love is higher, wider, deeper, infinitely MORE than this morphed example.*

Christ is the invisible God made visible, the heart of the Three-in-One's raw eternal love expressed to our world, infinitely and intricately present to every person who has ever been born and all those yet to be. They can be intimately, fully engaged with each individual *as if* we were the only person ever created. Touching the deepest part of our soul and knowing every possibility of every moment in our lives, every intersection with every other life—working to orchestrate all things to ensure that we experience Them, and the Truth about ourselves.

God orchestrates this experience with each person from birth to death and beyond—never sacrificing a single moment with anyone. This Love transcends mere individual interaction, as it also holds together and sustains the entire cosmos. The Divine is beyond the pictures we have in our minds, light-years above our limited ideas of Who They are.

God is **always greater** than the concepts we have about God.

Consider the following: at the moment you're reading this, the edge of the "observable universe" is approximately 92 billion light-years across. What does that even mean? We see the scientific explanation that it's the distance that a photon of light, traveling at 186,000 miles per second, travels in 92 billion years. But after a certain point, the number of zeros gets overwhelming to the point of mind-tilt, and the math becomes muddled and meaningless. We can write out the number and understand that it's gigantic beyond gigantic, but our minds have no valid reference point to put it in perspective. It's beyond anything our mental scales can measure.

Our projected image of human love in its most incredible form versus God's love is like comparing a single subatomic particle against the entire 92 billion light-years across the universe. Their love is the quantum field of energy that fills and connects every cubic millimeter in this universe and spills over into whatever is on the other side. According to the latest math and physics models, astrophysicists believe it consists of a series of additional universes that form the *multiverse*. We really can't attempt to comprehend any of this. Instead, we must gape with mouth and heart-eyes wide open into this mystery and possibility, and allow it to draw us in reverent astonishment before the Uncreated.

> *"And now here is my secret, a very simple secret. It is only with the heart that one can see rightly. What is essential is invisible to the eye."*
> **Antoine de Saint Exupery**[32]

God's Love is not a better version of human love; no matter how many thousands or millions or trillions of times, we magnify our highest examples. It is unfathomably ridiculous and infinite. *It is other*. Because God is other than we are—in essence, attributes, and expression; yet, They have chosen to focus the entire weight of Their love on you and me by including us into Themselves.

Ahhh now here's where we come to the fascinating and jaw-dropping plot twist...the mystery of God's "otherness," so far above and beyond us that it's incomprehensible, and yet closer than our breath...intimate lover, Abba Father, treasured Friend. What a beautiful, confusing mystery. And it's closer even than this! The God of the entire universe infuses Spirit-breath into the creatures They have made—Their image-bearers. In so doing, Christ has forever joined with us so profoundly that we can only frame it as Oneness. Union. Entanglement. At-One-Ment.

We are in Christ, and Christ is in us.
We share the sacred intimacy
within the Divine Flow.

God is altogether distinct and "other"...
yet, altogether "same."

This is nothing but an unbounded, unrestrained mystery. Your identity, right here right now, is that you are wholly, completely, relentlessly loved by the Creator of the galaxies and the Architect of your soul. They fashioned

---

32. Saint-Exupéry, Antoine, and Katherine Woods. *The Little Prince*, 1943. Print.

CHAPTER 9: IMPLICATION – CHRIST-EXPRESSION IN THE WORLD

you into Their image and likeness so that They can enjoy your existence in Them, and then deposited Their 92-billion-light-years-across Love into the depths of your being *by joining Themselves to you.*

This intense love is so intricate and tangibly persistent that it reaches into every subatomic particle within your heart, alters the chemical make-up of every cell, and invades every neuron and synapse within your mind. In other words, there is nothing and nowhere outside of the infinite reach of Their gentle, healing flow.

*Fully present. All of God. In you.
Right now.*

Are we able to grasp this? We must let Their Love wash through us, shape us, establish itself in the deepest part of our being and become the source of our life...our reason. They know, from Their vantage point deep within our spirit, every secret longing in our soul, every broken area and salty tear of sadness, every weakness and insecurity and fear, every haunting memory and recurring nightmare, every stray thought and rogue cancer cell and hint of shame. They have joined Themselves to all of who we are. They are experiencing the world through our soul and senses, intimately acquainted with our ways, familiar with every quark and quirk!

There is nothing hidden from the Relentless One, and They have faithfully committed with all that They are to complete the good work They began within us. As we give ourselves to this mystery, all that is **not true** begins to burn away in the presence of Their fiery, unconditional Love. Our True Self emerges from the ashes as untruth melts away.

This is who we are in Christ and Who They are in us. In Them, we find our rest and our real life. How do we reinforce this reality of our un-becoming so that we become convinced—fully persuaded—of our True Identity? We'll look at this in the next chapter.

Black Hole Takeaway from Implication

We are full-time, lifetime expressions of Christ in whatever situation we find ourselves in, because God has joined Themselves to us in the deepest part of our being.

Chapter 10
Instigation — Quantum Physics and the Kingdom
(Ephesians, Colossians)

Stick with me here through this chapter. It is longer than the others, as it takes some time to set the quantum stage for the payoff at the end. The framework of quantum physics allows us to see infinite possibilities when interacting with reality...the illusion of our Deepfake identity runs quite parallel to the illusion of the world that we live in. We believe the world is a separate, independent reality unaffected and disconnected from our observation of it. This couldn't be further from the truth.

Our Un-Becoming

The story goes that someone came upon Michelangelo staring intently at a block of marble, weighing well over six tons, and asked what he was doing. After a long pause, the artist replied that he was envisioning the sculpture that lay hidden within the stone and saw all that was *not* part of the finished piece that he would need to chip away. Two years later, he unveiled the masterpiece for the world to see—David, one of the most iconic pieces in all of art history. How? In simple terms, Michelangelo removed all the stone that was NOT David, so that the true image could emerge to match what had always been in his vision.

The work of the artist was to "release" David from its stone prison.

This is much like what God does with us.

INTO THE ABYSS

The Artist comes to release us from the prison of our Deepfake identity and free our True Self to emerge. The stone prison is mainly unknown to us, lying deep within our subconscious mind, but God will never lose sight of Their vision of who They created us to be. This is our "un-becoming."

But God does not come with a hammer and chisel. Instead, They come to us disguised as our own lives, using our own experiences (whether good, disastrous, ugly, painful, or glorious) to release our Real Self from our mind-prison.

We are in the process of becoming who we already are. Perhaps it's better to say that we are *un-becoming* all we are not. We are not known by our birth certificate, childhood memories, photos, current job, family situation, or image that stares back at us in the mirror. We are *more* than our name, our stuff, our thoughts, experiences, sensations, beliefs, or feelings. Maybe most importantly, we are *not* dirty, worthless sinners separated from a holy God because of our sin.

Our True Self was established before any of these things, and will outlast everything into the ages to come.

Perhaps this is a mostly unknown but critical aspect of the crucifixion that we saw way back in the pre-Creation Garden. It is a fierce stripping away and putting to death of all that we aren't. It is the ultimate un-becoming, the violent removal of all that is not true about us. To separate our True Self from the powerful influences of body and soul is no trivial task. It requires a painful death of sorts. Crucifixion of the Deepfake. Spaghettification of the false self. And it's an ongoing process as we continue growing into who we already are.

Remember...we are co-crucified with Christ. In black hole terminology, we are co-spaghettified with Christ. This is how God works to help us discover our True Self, extracting it from all the body and soul influences that have draped themselves over us as a "false self" throughout our history. One of the critical things that must be stripped away and buried forever is any hint of our separation from God because of something inherently flawed about our nature. This is a critical component that gives our Deepfake avatar its strength.

The surface version of "me," the one that's a compilation of everything in life that has led me to this present moment, is what I glimpsed when hurtling backward in time toward the black hole at the dawn of Creation. It included all the things I've done, stuff I've said, and the vast library of material containing all that others have done and said to me.

CHAPTER 10: INSTIGATION - QUANTUM PHYSICS AND THE KINGDOM

You and I are fantastic, drastic, spastic collages of our history and the history of all those that have gone before us. This is the seemingly obvious version of "us" that stares back in our mirrors each day and speaks convincingly from inside us to ourselves. They're bold and persuasive—these images, events, and voices that shape our self-image. There is a massive gravitational pull, primarily powered by our subconscious soul, to believe that this false self is who we really are. It provides us with a sense of comfort and security, and certainty. It's all we know, most of the time, and it projects a very convincing Deepfake. We'll get inside the workings of our subconscious shortly.

But the seemingly obvious version of me is *not* the real me. The real me, the one God has known from eternity past, is contained within my spirit. My True Self is not readily apparent when looking through natural eyes. Recall that I had received a revelation of my real life, God's union with me, through the eyes of a light-flooded spirit back in the pre-Creation Garden of Delights. My real life, buried beneath layers and layers of indoctrination that keeps my Deepfake thriving, is finally coming to the surface.

And what do I discover deep within, once my Deepfake is stripped away?

At the center of my being lies an uncreated, holy Christ-Mystery connecting my spirit to the Divine and all that exists. It is my true identity, assigned in my original birthplace, the Source of my authentic origin. I was designed as a spirit-being within a Singularity, to be an eternal recipient of God's great delight. I emerge as Their creative masterpiece, chiseled from the stone block of my self-constructed mind-prison, as spirit...and my soul begins to sing a song of freedom.

As God is the Ground of *all* being, my spirit is the ground of *my* being—the deep part of me joined directly to God. This is where I am aware of my thoughts, feelings, experiences, beliefs, sensations—but not defined by them. All of these things are "mine," but they are not "me." Suffice it to say that our spirit is far more than we might have imagined. Let's stay with this for a minute.

Blue Skies and Spirit-Awareness

Let's say you were outside on a warm spring day, lying in the grass and staring up at the sky. Clouds form fanciful shapes as they pass, accompanied by dozens of birds winging their way across the expanse. You hear the rumble of thunder in the distance, and soon a fierce storm rolls through, with torrential rain featuring furious flashes of lightning and ominous thunder crashes. Just in time, you manage to take cover under a nearby shelter, and after about 20 minutes of storm watching, the sun comes back out and chases it away.

As you continue to look upwards...do the clouds, birds, thunderstorm, and sunshine happen TO the sky, or IN the sky? Is the sky affected by those things taking place, or is the sky just the background against which they come and go? Picture for a moment the sky's perspective. What is the sky's state as the clouds form, the birds fly to and fro, the storm rolls through, and the sun comes back out? Can you imagine the sky being "aware" but completely unaffected by anything that takes place?

So it is with our spirit. It is aware of everything taking place in the body and soul, all the thoughts and feelings and sensations that come and go. It "observes" all these things from a completely objective, calm, and fully present perspective, knowing it was perfectly designed to do this from eternity past.

We use phrases like "my" body and "my" feelings and "my" personality all the time without a second thought. But who is "my"? Who is it that claims body, emotions, and character for itself? It's my spirit—the deep part of my being that is joined to God. I am not my body, feelings, or personality, yet I am fully present to them and aware of all that takes place within their realms of existence.

I am NOT my Deepfake identity. It is "mine," but it is not "me," no matter how convincing it has been or how long I've believed it. As Artist, God must do a deep work to chip and strip away those aspects propping up my false identity. And that's exactly what They do—from the inside out.

Notice that I used the phrase "my" spirit. OK...Here's the wild reality down in our core being. The deepest part of me, the Singularity that is my spirit, is Christ. Christ in me, the hope of glory. Not I, but Christ lives in me. Is it possible for us to grasp this? The One in Whom all things are held together and consist, the Garden of Being itself is so wonderfully everywhere that it appears to our limited awareness as if God is nowhere, and that's precisely the mind-twist. The very spirit-awareness through which we most often look outwards in our search for God is, in reality, the most significant confirmation of the Divine Presence as our spirit!

We might say it like this: God is so completely present, so near, so united, so entangled, so joined together with us that we can never place Them outside of our consciousness as an external entity that we can observe.

CHAPTER 10: INSTIGATION - QUANTUM PHYSICS AND THE KINGDOM

How is it possible to be aware of God's Being as if it were outside our being? Our union with God, our participation in Christ by the Spirit, is the deepest reality within us. When we turn inward and consider our awareness, we realize that Christ within us looks back at us—with an eternal promise to complete the work that They began.

> **1 John 4:13 (VOICE)** How can we be sure that He (Christ) *truly* lives in us and that we *truly* live in Him? *By one fact:* **He has given us His Spirit**.

I believe this is why it took Apostle Paul three years sitting alone in stunned silence, being taught by the Spirit in the Arabian Desert, before he dared to articulate these heavenly mysteries about humanity's connectedness and being-ness in the Universal Christ. Even the things he conveyed tend to be read these days in such a sanitized setting that we lose the utter shock and awe that he felt when God first revealed it to him. (See 1 Cor. 2:10-13, Col. 1:27, Col. 2:9-10, Gal. 2:20, Eph. 1:4-11.)

I am aware of my failures, achievements, fears, dreams, and disappointments…they exist in the spirit-sky of my awareness, along with everything that was said, all that was done, and everything that happened to me. Cruel words, betrayal, illness, divorce, financial devastation, abuse, and trauma might carry tremendous weight and influence inside my soul and body. Yet, my spirit is fully aware of these events while remaining completely unaffected and unphased by them.

The deep reality of my identity—my True Self—goes infinitely beyond the shallow veneer of "positive thinking" or "healthy self-image" techniques sold on late-night infomercials. In fact, most "positive thinking" strategies simply cover up a massive amount of "negative thinking" that lies underneath the veneer. This is different. It is not a parlor trick, and it is not a shallow covering. This is the mind-warping, soul-transforming, spirit-uplifting awareness of the ultimate reality that exists *as* the center of my very being. I am being invited to sense and experience Truth.

Let me share one last flashback to the pre-Creation realm, where my spirit-being was immersed in the reality of God. I was aware that I was innocent and holy, known fully and completely, loved unconditionally exactly as I am—sharing joyfully and effortlessly in the Divine Flow. I was intimately connected with everyone and everything in existence, filled with otherworldly peace and hope and confidence, free to be fully myself without any hint of shame or fear or hesitation. I was convinced of my unique role in the eternal story. Equipped with all of heaven's resources to express the reality of Christ, and excited beyond words to share the Spectacular News of God's eternal love with all I would encounter in my spheres of influence on the Creation side of this black hole.

Note: Sometimes, it's best to just sit in silence before this internal Mystery, knowing it is the deepest, truest part of my being. This is the "Christ in me, hope of glory" mystery...the "Not I, but Christ lives in me" truth...I'm still learning to rest in this Reality, for it births, defines, sustains, and carries me each and every moment.

REFLECTION...I need to see and tangibly experience my co-crucifixion (co-spaghettification) as a stripping away of all that I am not—all of my false identities. Abba, I need Your spaghettification process to become more than mental assent, more than a safe belief. I need to feel the intensity of it, the raw ferocity of my masks and false identities ripped off so that I am fully persuaded of the Reality at the center of my being...Christ.

Deep Breaths to Enter Your Center

The gravitational pull from the Christ-Singularity within us is nearly infinite, so it's somewhat surprising that we barely sense its draw toward our center. One would think that it would exert such massive force that we would have no choice but to be pulled inward to the truth of our inner being.

But there are other incredibly strong gravitational forces generated for the sake of our Deepfake identities that fight desperately for survival, and are often sufficiently able to keep us from feeling the weight of the spirit's intense inward pull. I've found that when we allow ourselves the gift of silence, and mix in a few activating ingredients after we have quieted our mind and heart, we can often experience the beautiful draw of Christ into the depths of our spirit. This is where we prepare to be fully immersed into our True Selves...to bring the full weight of our being to the surface of our lives.

Let's try it! Find a place of solitude where you won't be interrupted, get into a relaxed position, close your eyes in hushed silence, and take a series of long, deep breaths. (Flashback to the Prologue: 11-second breaths – four-three-four.) Go ahead and take your time. There's no rush. As you breathe, imagine slowly, steadily sinking down past your physical senses,

CHAPTER 10: INSTIGATION - QUANTUM PHYSICS AND THE KINGDOM

past your soul with all its thoughts and emotions and beliefs and stresses, all the way down into your spirit, until you reach the Divine space that lies deep within you.

The center point of your being, the infinitely small "Singularity" at your core, is a wormhole to the pre-Creation Divine Sanctuary that birthed your existence. There is overflowing, unusual peace in this realm of shared, deep connection you have with God and with all other image-bearers. You are fully yourself here, *without* the influences of body and soul.

Even huge ships may be threatened by the gigantic waves that rise during a tropical storm at the ocean's surface. But if we were to dive down 250 feet, the sea is strangely quiet, strangely calm. In precisely the same way, this place of unusual calm lies deep within me. Christ-in-me is my true identity, and silence is the language that grants access to this realm, amidst the cacophony of noises competing for our attention. Always, in any moment, we can dive to that place deep within our spirit and find our True Self in perfect peace.

We shouldn't be surprised or alarmed when our soul feels the fury of the world's raging waves. Jesus Himself warned that we would face things that threaten to drown us, hurt us, overcome us. But take heart. Deep within lies our uncreated spirit, our unique expression of the Divine Breath. It is not affected by the noise, chaos, and violence around us, nor the sensations in our physical body; not even the reckless messes swirling in our own soul. My spirit is the calm lying under the deep ocean when storms are whipping up the surface waves into a frenzy. It is the unaffected sky of my being, against which the storm rages and dumps its fury, all the while remaining aware, present, and tuned in.

When my soul is troubled, I remember that my thoughts and emotions are *mine,* but they are not **me**. I am aware of the crashing waves at the surface, but they cannot reach down and touch the uncreated part of my being. I know the chaos of those things around me and inside me, but in the silence, I listen for the Voice within that reminds me of the greater Truth, the greater Story. As I continue focusing my mind, emotions, and will inward toward the realm of the spirit, the influence of Divine Flow weaves its way through my soul, leaving its imprint on the many ways I respond and express this reality into my life and the world around me.

INTO THE ABYSS

The Spirit of God is the Almighty's breath, and every time I inhale and exhale, I reinforce and remind my soul of my union with God—the entangled swirl of my spirit with Their Spirit. When I forget, when my soul is pummeled by voices and circumstances that tell me otherwise, I breathe deeply...and remember who I am. I enter my center until I experience the flow of the Divine. This is the Self I can bring with confidence in my life. This True Self also can see the world as it actually is, not just as it appears.

> *Every breath is a confirmation of my union with the Divine.*

Neo, the Matrix, and God's Kingdom

The world that we see is the world as it is. This is what we've learned as an indisputable fact. But what if this is the ultimate illusion? Our brains are incredibly complex "reality-creating" machines that serve up experiences brought to us by our physical senses...which we then assume are true without question.

In our traditional way of thinking, the external world operates by deterministic, mathematical laws. I, as the experiencer, am entirely separate from what I'm experiencing. I am simply the observer and cannot change anything about what I see.

As we explore with childlike eyes, I believe that quantum physics, general relativity, and the many cutting-edge innovators seeking to merge the best aspects of these sciences will lead us into better ways of understanding and engaging with what Jesus called "the Kingdom of God." It's been said that quantum physics is the physics of possibilities, because when we zoom down into the tiniest elements of our universe, we find that subatomic particles don't "exist" as we've previously understood this to mean. Instead, math and physics show us that these particles "exist" as *possibilities*, and it is the *observation of them* that transforms them into an experience of reality. It's a deeper-level understanding of that phrase from the Talmud we saw at the very beginning – "we see the world...not as IT is... but as WE are."

This leads us to a mind-jarring conclusion: the world "out there" is not independent of my own experience—it is intricately and powerfully connected.

CHAPTER 10: INSTIGATION - QUANTUM PHYSICS AND THE KINGDOM

I picture Neo, the lead character from the movie *The Matrix,* as he learns that he has been living his whole life in a computer-simulated world, a convincing 3D hologram, much like the modern world is to our unsuspecting minds. A group of rebels busts him out of this simulation, and he starts to learn the real-world rules from his mentor, a man named Morpheus. Neo then grows steadily in his ability to engage in the "simulated" world called the Matrix, where most humans aren't aware they live in a false reality. It's stunning to watch our hero learn that the Matrix's standard rules no longer applied once he armed himself with an awareness of true Reality. He doesn't "pray" for help after a certain point—he simply applies what he has gained from his time with Morpheus in the real world to the situations before him and sees the possibility of incredible influence as he grows into his True Self.[33]

If you haven't seen this movie, I wholeheartedly recommend it, and if you've seen it, maybe watch it again—with a new lens. As some have said, and I believe accurately, it is not just a sci-fi action-adventure film with legendary fight scenes—it is a brilliant documentary of our world. The ways of God, which I believe are hidden in plain sight in the Creation, are uncovered like never before as we continue to explore and discover new aspects of Reality.

We give ourselves the greatest possibility of ushering in the Kingdom of God, filled with righteousness, peace, joy, and harmony, by remembering the innocence and curiosity of our childhood and looking at both our world and the image-bearers that inhabit it, with those same eyes. I believe as we do this, Spirit will continue to unlock the endless mysteries of Christ in ways that allow us to engage Creation equipped with rules from another (heavenly) realm, just as Neo did in *The Matrix*. Remember, heaven (the real world) isn't some distant place beyond Pluto. Instead, it's the unseen but very present dimension of the Divine, one that can only be experienced with a heart of childlike faith.

---

33. Matrix. Directed by Andy Wachowski and Larry Wachowski, performances by Keanu Reaves, Laurence Fishburne, and Carrie-Anne Moss, Warner Bros, 1999.

INTO THE ABYSS

A Blockbuster Movie Hidden in Our Subconscious Mind

*"I am the Vine, you are the branches.
Those who remain in me, and I in them,
will produce much fruit."*

Jesus[34]

*Where does the Vine end
And the branches begin?
They are joined together…
United. One. Entangled.*

In a sense, they're one Living Organism. But most of us have such a hard time experiencing this as the truth. If we are designed to live and see from our True Self, why does it feel so impossible to "arrive"? Even when we discover the truth that Christ is our life, why do we end up living as if our body-and-soul false self is so obviously the real thing instead? We seem to default back to patterns with a hidden power, an extreme "gravitational pull" that we're not even aware of.

Well…that's EXACTLY what's happening.

Recent neurological research has shown that our body sends a little over 11 million bits of information per second to the brain for processing:[35]

- **Eyes** - 10 million bits/sec
- **Skin** – 1 million bits/sec
- **Ears and Nose** – every 100,000 bits/sec
- **Mouth** – 1,000 bits/sec

Millions of tiny pieces of information (bits) are being sent to the brain constantly, but the conscious mind is only capable of handling around 50 bits/second. This is the part of your mind that you use to read and process these words. As you look at this page, you are saying the words in your mind,

---

34. Jesus. NLT Bible, John 15:10
35. Carroll, Michael July 2008 "Understanding Your Mind." NLP Academy, July 2008, accessed Jan 12.2020. https://www.nlpacademy.co.uk/articles/view/understanding_your_mind_conscious_and_unconscious_processing/

CHAPTER 10: INSTIGATION - QUANTUM PHYSICS AND THE KINGDOM

deriving meaning from the text, and establishing how it relates to you. Your conscious mind is linear, sequential, and logical, trying to figure it all out and get everything to make sense. Here's the problem: *most* of what's going on inside your brain lies underneath your conscious awareness.

The unconscious mind is everything else in the soul and body system that is not conscious at that moment. We can say that the unconscious mind has complete knowledge of the system that is you, and it manages most of it in autopilot mode. Your breathing, your heartbeat, your blinking, and the control of the overall operation of your many trillion cells are all functioning under the radar of your logical mind.

Your unconscious mind also has phenomenal processing capabilities compared with the conscious mind. The subconscious can handle up to *20 million bits per second* compared to the painfully "slow" 50 bits per second or so in the conscious. This means something like 400,000 movies can be playing in our minds at any one time, and we'd only be aware of one of them!!

What's in those movies playing in our sub-consciousness?

Well, remember when I was hurtling backward in time and space toward the Alpha-point Singularity, and I was catching strobe-like glimpses of my entire history? Most of those glimpses of information are stored somewhere in my subconscious mind, remaining hidden for the most part in my day-to-day life. These bits of information are being continuously processed by my brain to bring me what I experience as "reality"...who I believe I am, and my role in the disconnected world around me, the world that my senses are telling me is real.

My stored memories, sensations, fears, traumas, inner vows, core beliefs, and subjective map of reality are all part of a lifetime of subtle subconscious "programming" inside my mind's deep neural network. And it has slowly, steadily created my convincing false self-identity. This internal algorithm wars against anything that might threaten the survival of my Deepfake, which loves the perceived comfort, safety, and certainty of life within the Matrix...especially if everything in life seems to be humming along without significant issues. Anything that threatens my comfortable existence in this false world sets off loud warning bells in my mind, sending the soul into attack or distract mode to subdue and eliminate (or avoid and numb) any intruding thoughts.

INTO THE ABYSS

These pre-programmed false self-affirming movies are continually playing in my mind's background, unknown to the conscious me, but firmly shaping my identity and reinforcing my mirage-life in the world. The sources of this fake persona are so deeply hidden that I'm not even aware that I'm living as a Deepfake body-and-soul avatar inside an even more convincing Deepfake illusion of the world around us. Most of what resides in my subconscious mind reinforces the counterfeit, separated self that hides my true nature and veils the way I see.

Most...but not all.

Here's the thing: There's a deep place within our subconscious mind that *knows* that it knows that it knows our union with God and our connection to the Creation. It knows its True Identity and origin and understands that the world created by our senses is a convincing illusion. But our conscious mind, with its multiple filters and biases, doing its level best to concentrate and organize its inner and outer world, keeps this fundamental truth buried and hidden in the subconscious. It then focuses on remaining safe and comfortable and separate inside the world we're used to seeing. We are designed and wired to know our Real Self in and as Christ, but this information is difficult to market and sell to our logical brain.

Our massive struggle then is to harness this Truth from the dark basement of our subconscious and lead it up the stairs into the light of our conscious awareness. This is no easy task! To cue up and watch the One Movie inside us that's accurately displaying the Truth of our being and the illusion of the Matrix, we need to first observe from the right frame of reference.

There may be 399,999 movies playing inside our subconscious minds that reinforce our separated false self and the simulation Matrix. Still, a spectacular internal film shows us our True Self, which is more powerful and carries more influence than all the others combined. It's a movie that all of us have within us. It is directed by Abba in heaven, produced by Christ, and deposited into you by the Spirit before your birth. It's called the Christ Story, and it's playing inside all of us now. Our challenge is to find that movie, hit "play," and put it on "repeat" until it changes the way we perceive, believe, and interact with our world. As Paul writes to the Corinthians, "**We have** *the mind of Christ*, and hold the thoughts, feelings and purposes of His heart" (see I Cor 2:16). In other words, we are *participants in Divine Consciousness*.

CHAPTER 10: INSTIGATION - QUANTUM PHYSICS AND THE KINGDOM

Frame of Reference

At this moment, you probably aren't aware that you're hurtling through space at ridiculous speeds, especially if you're sitting in a cozy chair or lying on a couch. It feels like you're entirely at rest. But in reality the earth itself is spinning on its axis at 1000 miles per hour, while it orbits the sun at 67,000 mph, while our solar system orbits the Milky Way galaxy at 490,000 mph, and our whole galaxy moves toward a distant structure in outer space at 1.3 million mph. It's a wonder we don't fly off the earth as we travel at those mind-bending speeds! But since we are moving at the same rate as the planet, then as long as the earth is our "frame of reference," it appears that we are at rest.

For example, if I were traveling in a car at 88 mph, and the vehicle is my frame of reference, I am at rest—since I'm also traveling at 88 mph. An observer sitting in the car with me would measure my speed relative to them as zero mph. Now, if the ground is my reference instead—for instance if a stationary police car hiding by the road as I drove by measured my speed—I'd be clocked with a radar gun at 88 mph. And he wouldn't likely let me off, even if I told him I was speeding because I was *really* craving a frozen Mountain Dew. Make sense? We calculate our speed in relation to what we use as our frame of reference.

It's the same way when we "calculate," or perceive, our identity. It's completely dependent on our frame of reference—the perspective of the observer. When our frame of reference is the "mind of the world"—a self-centered perception of reality, primarily rooted in the experiences of our physical senses—we see and operate from a sense of separation from God and others. Our frame of reference is limited to our bodies and souls, with strict lines all around us demarcating *us vs. them*. Our Deepfake fully believes that it needs to struggle and carve out its personal meaning in this harsh, disconnected world. This fallen frame of reference is what powers our false identity.

But when our frame of reference is the "mind of Christ"—a God-centered perception of reality—we see and operate from a sense of entanglement with God and others. We are no longer separate from the world that we are experiencing. Our identity is Christ, and there is only "us" and no "them." We can then become grateful participants in the quantum field that permeates the universe, joining all things together in a cohesive flow that issues forth from the One. This takes us back to the color waves we saw in the pre-Creation, flowing from the pure white holographic light of Christ's love throughout the Garden of Delights.

It's easy to see that waves are part of the ocean because our minds are programmed to perceive the fluidity of water. It's the same with branches on a vine. But what about the connection between a person, a plant, and a planet? We just don't have the means to "see" the universe-filling ocean of energy on which people, pandas, plants, and planets are all waves—each having its own experience of existence in the Matrix. To see these as joined in the same way is not intuitively evident, because our minds are programmed from birth onward to see them as obviously separate.

Quantum physics is changing the rules, though. Down at the subatomic level, there are little wave/particle packets of energy (called "quanta"), which are spinning like mini whirlwinds and pinging in and out of existence. This has brought a radical reframe to our perceptions of reality.

This area of quantum physics demonstrates that everything in existence is entangled—energetically connected in the quantum field—because it was once contained within the infinitely small Singularity when the universe began. Our ancient spiritual traditions, including Jesus Himself, tell us that we are all joined together by our participation as branches on a Vine—the Source that connects and sustains the entire universe in Christ.

We're finally starting to see and believe what Jesus meant when He talked about our participation in the Kingdom of Heaven, which He described as being both within us *and* all around us. Science isn't using this same language, but notice that this is the same reality described as we explore the wonders of the quantum field. This reality integrates our inner world with our outer world, connecting us with the Creation on a level deeper than we could have ever imagined.

*We are **CREATING** the world by the way we choose to **SEE** the world.*

The Kingdom Jesus spoke of involved a way of seeing the world—God, others, ourselves—as connected, as One. A world where serving the "least of these" is serving Christ directly. It sees Love as the binding agent that holds it all together, as well as the healing agent for the damage caused when we mistakenly see ourselves through the eyes of our false, separated

CHAPTER 10: INSTIGATION - QUANTUM PHYSICS AND THE KINGDOM

selves. This "Kingdom of God" and the "quantum field" are both referring to our deeply connected, entangled world—which we'll never enter with our whole being unless we commit with childlike hearts to a new way of seeing and being.

Maybe it's better that scientists often aren't aware that the wisdom of ancient spiritual traditions is affirmed by the beautiful, interconnected realities they are discovering as they explore the universe. I think this keeps the research authentic and unbiased. Some folks may be furious that the most recent scientific findings are simply confirmations of our Christ-soaked, entangled world—the existence of the Kingdom of God that Jesus came to help us unveil.

With Christ as our frame of reference, we can finally begin to see what's true.

Shared Atoms

The human body is an amazing mix of science and art, a living expression of Divine Breath that has become aware of its existence. The Psalmist rejoiced that he was "knit together in his mother's womb, fearfully and wonderfully made" in God's very image (see Ps. 139). What a joy to be an expression of God on the earth!

> *"The glory of God is man, fully alive."*
> Iranaeus[36]

We each have about 100 trillion cells in our body, and each cell contains nearly 100 trillion atoms, each one a mini-universe within itself.[37] Every breath we take contains about 25 sextillion molecules—that's 10 with 21 zeros after it. What's stunning and incomprehensible is that all of these atoms inside you at this very moment may well have been part of volcanoes, rivers, giant oak trees, a brontosaurus, diamonds, jungles, pyramids, and people who lived in the first century. For certain, your carbon atoms saw the inside of a distant star, survived a tremendous explosion, and sailed through the universe to arrive at earth and end up inside of you. Wow!!

---

36. Iranaeus. *Against Heresies*, Book 4, Chapter 34, Section 7. Oxford: Clarendon Press, 1874.
37. Dr. Ananya Mandal, MD News-Medical.Net, Sept 26, 2018 accessed May 10,2020 https://www.news-medical.net/news/20180926/Mapping-the-trillions-cells-in-the-human-body.aspx

INTO THE ABYSS

Mathematically speaking, making a few basic assumptions about how atoms are distributed across the globe, there is a high probability that we have within us at any moment, the same atoms that have been inside **every other person** who has ever lived. At the atomic level, then, our physical beings are actually a part of each other. When we think about it, this is quite amazing! Even more remarkable is the metaphysical reality at the subatomic level that joins us even more intricately. At our core, we are entangled with everything that exists as participants in the quantum field—waves of possibility on the ocean of the Divine.

Eternal Seeds of Possibility

Our inner universe contains a Singularity, which is Christ. This reality is the deepest core of our being and cannot change. Once we allow ourselves the gift of childlike faith to dive into this center space within us and soak inside it for a while, we see that our lives, and all that we express into the world, are "seeds of possibility."

Just as we are only in our infancy when it comes to our experiential understanding of God, we are also just barely starting to grasp the immensity of the inner universe within our being. We are each a riddle wrapped in a mystery covered by counterfeit concepts of separation, fear, and shame that haven't allowed us to explore the depths of what it means to be human. To be fully ourselves. To carry the authority of being a Christ-expression.

But there's hope. More and more are starting to see. Many are throwing off religious chains that have bound us to tribal ways of seeing God and being human, and momentum is forming around a renewed vision for the world. We are shedding counterfeit concepts, unwrapping interior mysteries, and addressing inner riddles that unlock our identity and purpose. When we finally get a glimpse, we are shocked and delighted at what we find looking back at us from the deepest core of our being...*Christ, the hope of glory.*

When we combine our seeds of possibility with those of others, planted in the fertile soil of the Garden of Delights (G.o.D.), we magnify the impact and influence of God's love. Because Christ is the Singularity at the center of my being and the center of your being, we are Spirit-entangled at the deepest possible level—deep calling unto deep. A flow of love and unity is present between those aware of their connection in Christ. When we express this love, we replicate a scenario similar to black holes colliding and merging into one.

CHAPTER 10: INSTIGATION - QUANTUM PHYSICS AND THE KINGDOM

When this cosmic collision occurs in outer space, the singularities combine into one. The mass and density increase exponentially, and its gravitational pull toward the center is magnified. What that means for us here on earth, in black hole terms, is that when we are expressing love toward others who embrace a shared vision with us, this same cosmic collision occurs between our inner spaces. Christ-in-me collides with Christ-in-you, and our inner singularities effectively combine into one.

This serves to expand and extend the event horizon around the combined Christ-Singularity formed from our "collision" with our brothers and sisters. Just like when black holes merge, the "gravitational pull" toward Christ increases on *all* those within our spheres of influence, becoming an invitation for them to experience the reality of God, dive into the mystery, and discover their True Selves.

And we're about to see that our spheres of influence carry far greater possibilities than we've imagined...

Holograms – Slices of Reality

Remember those holograms that were popular back in the 1980s? I had several of them on stickers, bookmarks, and a few of my baseball cards. They're still around today—on driver's licenses, credit cards, medical records, and the like. It's a laser-etched 2D image appearing in 3D when moved back and forth under the right conditions. What's fascinating is that if you cut out a small piece of the 2D hologram, the entire 3D image remains encoded within it, and you can still see the whole thing. The same concept can be replicated with a laser and mirrors, producing a three-dimensional holographic display, as we saw in the pre-Creation Garden. This display can often be so convincing that it appears to be a solid object.

Imagine their surprise when scientists, studying black holes' specific behavior, found that the universe operates on a similar principle because of our entanglement within the quantum field.[38] *The whole is mirrored in the fragment.* In other words, if we keep dividing up the universe into smaller and smaller sections, each tiny section still contains information within it that mirrors the whole. They first discovered this mathematically by recognizing that there was information "frozen" at the event horizon surrounding a black hole—a 2D representation of all the 3D information

---

38. Bekenstein, Jacob D. *Information in the Holographic Universe*, Scientific American, https://www.scientificamerican.com/article/information-in-the-holographic-univ/ April 1, 2007. accessed April 17, 2020

they previously thought had disappeared inside the Singularity. And the entire holographic "display" of what we know as our universe is being projected from a Single Source...the Ultimate Observer. We know this Observer as Christ.

Now, there are many complex reasons behind how and why this is the case. What it means in context is that our participation in our tiny part of the universe has significant influence and impact on the whole. When we operate from the True Self with grace, wisdom, and honor, we deposit "seeds of possibility" into our given portion of the holographic universe. And each small seed bends the arc of the whole toward healing and wholeness. This means every random act of kindness, every warm thought, every encouraging word, every good intention, every hand raised to send healing has effects infinitely beyond what's visible or known to us in our little corner of the galaxy.

Butterflies in Brazil and Tornados in Texas

In 1961, a meteorology professor at MIT named Edward Lorenz coined the term "butterfly effect" while studying weather patterns using highly complex computer simulations.[39] His discovery that small changes in nature can have enormous consequences became a powerful insight that went far beyond just predicting the weather. It ended up expanding into what we know today as chaos theory. The iconic idea that became wildly popular from this research went something like this: the flap of a butterfly's wings in Brazil today can set off a tornado in Texas next week.

Well, pop culture ran with this "butterfly effect" concept to emphasize that seemingly insignificant actions can produce drastic effects. While this is true and important, Lorenz's central idea demonstrated that the future is not formulaic. It is, in fact, unpredictable. We can predict specific outcomes with a degree of probability, but because tiny changes can have huge effects, the future can't be predicted with any degree of certainty.

The future instead is packed with *potential and possibility*.

Interestingly, when you dive down into the subatomic world's inner workings, quantum physics tells us something very similar. Some particles seem to be popping in and out of existence at the electron-microscopic level and are only measurable when observed in a specific location. In other words, the way we measure the location of subatomic particles at

---

39. Dizikesarchive, Peter. *When the Butterfly Effect Took Flight,* MIT Technology Review, https://www.technologyreview.com/2011/02/22/196987/when-the-butterfly-effect-took-flight/ February 22, 2011. Accessed May 20, 2020.

CHAPTER 10: INSTIGATION - QUANTUM PHYSICS AND THE KINGDOM

any moment in time is by the "probability" that they may be there—not by the certainty of where they are. Our *observation* of these particles directly affects their whereabouts and their dynamics. This is because when we observe a particle (reference: double-slit experiment), what is known as the particle's "wave function" (a "wave" of possibilities where the particle *might* be located) collapses and becomes measurable.[40]

Here's something else to ponder...every human being is 99.99999996% empty space.[41] We are SO non-solid that if all the open space is completely removed from every human being on the planet right now, calculations have shown that all seven-plus billion of us would fit into the size of a single piece of candy. And further still, inside each of those almost empty atoms, are subatomic particles, infinitely tiny packets of energy, whizzing around like mini-tornadoes at light-speed and pinging in and out of existence, to the point where the whole concoction is *essentially like a cloud of subatomic smoke*. There's literally nothing there to touch. It would make for a great science fiction episode on Star Trek, except...this is Reality.

All of this simply means that our thoughts, emotions, intentions, and voice generate frequencies and energy that affect particles' movement at the subatomic level. This happens in ways that were once thought to be in the realm of science fiction. But your spirit is indeed joined to Christ and carries the same creative force that spoke the universe into existence. Do you remember the earlier studies that revealed the effects our thoughts, meditation, and imagination can have on water, plants, eggs, vegetables, and sperm? If water responds to our words, and organisms respond to our imagination, how does the "world out there" respond to our inner consciousness? Virtually, all living cells "respond" to our stimuli because of the intricate universal connection that entangles all things within Creation.

You are filled with more possibilities and potential than you have ever dared to dream. The probability of your "butterfly effect" actions, ideas, feelings, and beliefs propels the world toward the Creation's ultimate dream (the Omega-point vision) every time you allow yourself to surrender to the Divine Flow and act out of your true nature. And it doesn't matter in the least that most of these seemingly tiny, insignificant things that you do may go almost entirely unnoticed.

---

40. Freiberger, Marianne *"Watch and Learn"*, +Plus Magazine, https://plus.maths.org/content/watch-and-learn Nov 20, 2016. Accessed July 20, 2020.

41. Helmenstine, Anne Marie, Ph.D. *"How Many Atoms Are There in a Human Cell?"* ThoughtCo, https://www.thoughtco.com/how-many-atoms-in-human-cell-603882 Feb 11, 2020. Accessed June 2, 2020

Suppose we combine the butterfly effect with the holographic effect in the quantum field that connects us with God and the Creation. In that case, we begin to see that our lives, thoughts, and voices carry infinitely more weight than most of us have ever realized. The butterfly effect says that a tiny stimulus can produce the possibility of a disproportionately large reaction. The holographic effect says that a stimulus entering the quantum field in my small part of the universe can influence the whole. Do you see the incredible potential here?!? Our thoughts, emotions, and intentions *in the current moment* carry factors of exponential multiplication beyond anything that science has previously thought possible. The *way* we see creates the *world* we see!

And that's all we really have, isn't it? The present moment, which is a true gift. The past doesn't exist, and the future doesn't exist yet. We live only in a string of moments. Our Deepfake false self is driven primarily by the algorithm in our subconscious—a good portion of which is filled with memories of the past and anxieties about the future. This is understandable, of course. I still struggle with this every day. It's the way of the world, and it seems so familiar, so necessary to frame our lives according to our clocks and calendars, to keep ourselves as comfortable and cozy as possible.

> *"The distinction between the past, present and future is only a stubbornly persistent illusion."*
> **Albert Einstein**[42]

But when our frame of reference is the "mind of Christ," and we learn to believe and operate in our True Self, we discover that all we have is this moment. We are in the midst of an eternal "now" with no beginning or end, just as I discovered in the pre-Creation Garden, where there was *no* sense of space or time, and the *possibilities were endless*.

The Power of Prayer

What comes to mind when you think of prayer? We've already talked about what I consider the *best* kind of prayer, which is when we "enter our center" and listen in silence. This is what I envision. But for many people, prayer primarily involves asking God for help.

---

42. Einstein, Albert. *Essays in Science*, Dover Publications; May 21, 2009, Dover ed.

CHAPTER 10: INSTIGATION - QUANTUM PHYSICS AND THE KINGDOM

Let's consider something other than our sincere "requests" for help and intervention to a God we perceive as distant and somewhat reluctant, which is the model of prayer I have known for most of my life. We have unwittingly created in our minds a deity that only answers "if it is His will" after we pray long enough, fervently enough, often enough, accompanied with appropriate scripture and fasting and prayer chains. This isn't what I'm going to suggest here. I believe we can enjoy the possibility of another way, something more raw and intimate and real.

In 1978, 7000 "expert" meditators collaborated in a controlled study, and were given instructions to spend their time focusing intently on thoughts of love and peace.[43] They did this for three weeks and measured statistics in several categories, including Crime, Health, Economy, Creativity, Education, and Safety.

Researchers then correlated this period to significant drops in global crime, notifiable diseases, suicide and infant mortality rates, alcohol and cigarette consumption, car crashes, and terrorist activity. At the same time, they noted increases in GNP (gross national product) per capita, patent applications, and marital stability. Because this was a highly controlled scientific experiment, global events, holidays, weather, and other variables were ruled out as contributors to the findings. As of 2017, over 50 such rigorous, peer-reviewed scientific studies into this phenomenon have been done, all utilizing time series analysis that controls for weekly trends and periodic cycles that influence social data.

We can expect this possibility when we join our spirit voice with the Voice of the Christ within us, when we speak the profound, universe-creating truth of our being into the quantum field with the full weight of our mind, emotions, convictions, and imagination all coming into play. It is the powerful tsunami that forms when our spirit swirls with Christ and enters boldly into the chaos of existence, witnessing the sheer force of love, bending the chaos toward wholeness, healing, peace, and connection.

This...is our sacred calling as co-creators with God, deep calling unto deep, unfolding the story of our original identity and our ultimate destiny.

---

43. Dillbeck, Michael C., Cavanaugh, Kenneth L. Sage Journals, *Societal Violence and Collective Consciousness: Reduction of U.S. Homicide and Urban Violent Crime Rates*, https://journals.sagepub.com/doi/full/10.1177/2158244016637891 ,April 14, 2016, accessed July 19, 2020.

INTO THE ABYSS

A Good God and a Good Creation

From modern advances in biology, we know that a new thought pattern takes several years to be fully formed in the brain, creating essentially a new chemical and physical "infrastructure" that enables an entirely different way of thinking. For years, I was a student of the great revivals and awakenings throughout history, and nearly every example I'm familiar with has been short-lived, not enough time for thought patterns to align with a new definition of "normal."

These revivals were often centered in a Gospel that heavily emphasized God's holy perfection against our utter worthlessness and wretched sinfulness—a message fueled by shame and fear—a fragile foundation that features fundamental flaws. This fear-and-shame message has provided lasting strength to the "worldly mind" that birthed our Deepfake identities, while burying our true ones under layers upon layers of religious and cultural stone. It's sad and eye-opening to have learned that most of our famous revivals have been very successful inoculations against the experience of our True Selves.

Consider for a minute the possibility that God has entrusted the future of the earth into *our* hands. We're told in the scriptures that the "creation is groaning to see the sons of God manifest in the earth" (Rom. 8:19). The world is straining, teeth clenched under the weight of a cruel unreality, waiting in anguished anticipation for those who have seen the spectacular vision of Christ-in-all to unshackle it and reveal the hidden glory of God's universe and our participation within it.

We live in a world that received the highest God-blessings possible—a series of proclamations during each step of Creation that "it is good," all culminating in a magnificent declaration once the first image-bearer was formed: "It is VERY good!" But, understandably, we don't see everything around us as "very good" today. Some might even say that the world looks like it's going to hell in a handbasket, and things have never been worse.

What do we do then, when we look out at our illusory world suffering such agony under the cruel weight of violence, addiction, pain, disharmony, and destruction? All deeply rooted in our perceived separation from God and each other, trapping us in a seemingly downward cycle of futility and decay? Only when we arm ourselves with an unwavering vision of our glorious True Self can we embrace, without blinking, the inherent goodness

CHAPTER 10: INSTIGATION - QUANTUM PHYSICS AND THE KINGDOM

of both the Creator and the Creation as we stare directly into the dragon's lair of our world...A realm filled with the grotesque horror of conflict, abuse, and death.

It takes a foolish and furious resolve to cling to a vision of a good God and a good Creation when standing in the middle of multiple hells. The evening news blares non-stop messages of a world gone mad, so is it any wonder that so many believe that this world system has no hope for peace and harmony without outside intervention?

Our world is experiencing various degrees of alienation with God and each other, but this is not the final word. It cannot be. Maybe when we permit ourselves to see humans as the God-breathed expressions of Christ that they truly are, we might find the incredible audacity to courageously enter our suffering world and treat each other as intricately connected in Christ. Divine image-bearers of unsurpassable worth.

A lofty view of God requires a lofty view of humanity. Only as we embrace a vision of human goodness can we courageously battle our world's intense ugliness with a fierce and holy rage. We are piercing through the illusions with swords of Truth, calling our planet to realize and embrace its Original Identity as we hurtle together toward the eschaton.

A Vision for Our Inner Universe

Can we see Christ in ourselves and each other? Is it genuinely possible to look underneath our Deepfake avatars and see our breathtaking True Selves, our interconnected spirits in Christ? I'm not asking whether we acknowledge it or understand it, or nod our head vigorously in agreement with the concept. Can we set aside what we think we know, what we've been trained and programmed to believe for so many years, and sink down into our spirit to *see with the eyes of God*?

I tend to gravitate towards intellectual understanding, trying to carefully study these topics to articulate the intersection of science and theology in a way that makes logical sense. But this isn't what we need here. What we need instead is a head-on collision with the Truth of our identity that rips the false "us" away from our real selves and allows us to encounter Christ within us as our identity. Spaghettify me, dear God!!

I'll repeat it because I need this for myself, and I cannot overstate its importance. *Agreeing that my identity is in Christ is NOT the same as encountering Christ AS my identity.* No matter how profound, our understanding of a concept can easily become a vaccination against the Reality's full experience behind the idea. For example, when you get a measles shot, the nurse injects a tiny bit of the measles into your arm so that your body can manufacture its immunity to the full-blown experience of the disease. Our minds do the same thing with the concept of our identity. We inject a little dose of understanding, and our minds manufacture their immunity to the full-blown experience of the Reality. Our false selves continue on autopilot, mostly oblivious to the universe-bending Reality of Christ at the center of our being.

Here's a strange suggestion: I'm not sure this concept of our True Identity can be taught. It must be received, I think, by a work of God within us. But this is Their great delight! It is God's will and good pleasure to offer us the Kingdom in all its fullness and to affirm our true identity—which then enables us to experience the Garden of Delights within our soul. What joy rushes through us when we discover the tangible reality of Christ as our Life, and our growing wide-eyed recognition that this is true for all who bear Their image.

I believe that healthy meditation can position us for an encounter that imparts this to our inner being, especially if the right elements are present within our imagination. Often, either great suffering or great love can position us for this type of head-on collision with truth as well. But in the end, I don't think there are any easy, magic formulas.

Science and metaphysics can present an abundance of clues for us, but they alone cannot generate a compelling interior vision that connects us intimately to God's desire and power. We can learn that the universe was contained in a Singularity, and everything is intricately connected and sustained within the unified field. That "matter" as we know it is better described as mainly empty whirling tornadoes of infinitely small waves of energy, and that all of existence is a holographic projection of Divine Consciousness. However, these facts can swirl uselessly in the realm of our intellect, collecting brain-dust and accomplishing nothing. We need an "activating agent" for these facts to intermingle and explode into a life-giving inner vision.

Something must supply the *"oomph"* to fully persuade us, once and for all, that God IS good, that God's Creation IS good, and that everything is intricately connected both to God and each other. Thankfully, it's the

CHAPTER 10: INSTIGATION - QUANTUM PHYSICS AND THE KINGDOM

Spirit at the core of our being Who can accomplish this. When we take the right ingredients, mix them within our active imagination, and visualize what is True—Christ in all—we can learn to look at our world, peel back the convincing "unreality" layers of the Matrix, and see underneath with Divine eyes. Like Neo when he sees the programmed "code" of the Matrix, there is a confidence and unshakeable holy power that rises within us when we look—*with the spirit-eyes of the Real World*—at the unreal world we inhabit.

When we see this way, we will never again be able to unsee.

This holy confidence cannot arise by merely hearing someone else tell us what's true. It must come from *within* us. Neo, in *The Matrix*, didn't arise in power from words that were spoken by those around him. At a critical juncture in the story, he paused, listened to the inner voice, and realized what he truly believed. This began his awakening into his True Self...and this is our journey as well.

The Spirit of God within us is the activating agent that aligns our mind, emotions, and intentions to call forth this Reality, to speak and act with the courage of Christ-within-us, helping free ourselves and those in our spheres from the multitude of distracting voices dousing us with deception. Voices all around us continuously and convincingly reinforce our counterfeit stories of separation that prop up our Deepfake selves and our Deepfake Matrix world, leading humanity further and further down a path of conflict, pain, and disharmony. But the Voice that called Creation into being, resides within you as your identity, and speaks of endless possibilities available to you in the present moment. Never forget this.

Many believers are waiting anxiously for a distant God to show up in great dominating power at some unknown point in the future and fix all that's wrong in the world. What if instead, They are waiting for *us* to rise up as expressions of Their great love, fueled by a compelling interior vision for the restoration of all things? What if the awareness of our Christ-identity empowers us with tenacious solidarity for the world, and carries transformational power to melt away its veiled unreality?

What if we don't make it to "heaven" unless everyone makes it there from God's perspective? Would that change the way we see and interact? And remember, let's frame heaven not as a post-death departure to a distant destination beyond Pluto, but as a realm of awakening to our True

Selves, and a new way of seeing our connection with God and each other. This is how we reveal glimpses of the Real World's glorious Kingdom that is steadily spreading to cover the whole earth, like the waters cover the sea.

The phenomenal unveiling of Christ-in-us and us-in-Christ is the revival we've been seeking.

Eph. 1:9-11 (VOICE) He has enlightened us to the great mystery at the center of His will. With immense pleasure, He laid out His intentions through Jesus, a plan that will climax when the time is right as He returns to create order and unity—both in heaven and on earth—when all things are brought together under the Anointed's royal rule. In Him we stand to inherit even more. As His heirs, we are predestined to play a key role in His unfolding purpose that is energizing everything to conform to His will.

Jude 1:24-25 (VOICE) Now to the One who can keep you upright and plant you firmly in His presence—clean, unmarked, and joyful in the light of His glory—to the one and only God, our Savior, through Jesus the Anointed our Lord, be glory and greatness and might and authority; just as it has been since before He created time, may it continue now and into eternity. Amen.

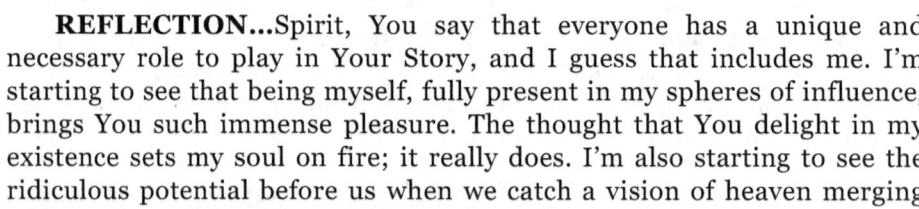

REFLECTION...Spirit, You say that everyone has a unique and necessary role to play in Your Story, and I guess that includes me. I'm starting to see that being myself, fully present in my spheres of influence, brings You such immense pleasure. The thought that You delight in my existence sets my soul on fire; it really does. I'm also starting to see the ridiculous potential before us when we catch a vision of heaven merging with earth, and You have laid out clues all over the cosmos to help us see this.

CHAPTER 10: INSTIGATION - QUANTUM PHYSICS AND THE KINGDOM

I don't want to be limited by how I've understood things in the past. My soul is a blank whiteboard, on which I grant You unlimited freedom to paint beautiful and convincing imagination-portraits that fuel my thoughts, feelings, intentions, and actions, giving them a supernatural, creative force to shape the reality of our universe. I am a Divine seed of unlimited possibility. Help me to see.

Black Hole Takeaways from the Quantum Field

- When we see that we are Divine seeds of possibility, we can engage with the quantum field of our world with a holy confidence that has the power to expose lies and reveal the true nature of Reality.
- Maybe instead of waiting for God to come and fix the world, They are waiting for us to live from our True Self...to bring the full weight of being into our spheres of influence.

Chapter 11
Impartation – The Omega-Point
(Revelation)

Traditionally, Jesus as the Alpha and Omega refers to the Creation and to the end times. Adding a little bit of nuance to fit what we've seen with black holes, we'll look at the three singularities that frame the eternal story of Christ.

Inner Abyss: Connecting Point between the Alpha and Omega

The first is the Original Creation event signifying the beginning (Alpha-point), and the second is the New Creation that God is bringing forth as the story closes (Omega-point). The third and central Singularity—the connection point between the other two—is now contained in our spirit's deep inner universe. This Christ-Singularity at our center joins us to the pre-Creation Divine Sanctuary before the story begins and to the New Creation reality at the end of the story.

- When we sink into the center of our internal Christ-Singularity and enter the reality on the pre-Creation side of the beginning black hole (the Alpha-point), we experience the love that begins all things. Our spirit and soul resonate with the **identity that comes from being included in the Divine sanctuary, animated by God's very Spirit-breath.**

- When we sink into the center of our internal Christ-Singularity and enter the reality on the brand-New Creation side of the ending black hole (the Omega-point), we experience the love that concludes all things. Our spirit and soul resonate with the **purpose that comes from being included in the story of God involving the entire Cosmos.**

Christ resides deep within the core of our being. God and Creation intertwine harmoniously within *US*, expressing the glory of Their dreams for us, as us. *WE* are the point of connection between the Alpha-point and the Omega-point, joining past and future reality in the present moment of our existence. *WE* are the Body of Christ on the earth, and hopefully, we can see now that this is far more than just a nice analogy. We **ARE** God expressing Themselves through our humanity into the holographic quantum field that permeates our planet, what Jesus called the Kingdom of Heaven. *WE* are the Story of Christ.

> *We are each unique, necessary expressions of Christ in our spheres of influence.*

Is. 65:17 (Voice) Eternal One: Now look here! I am creating new heavens and a new earth. The *weary and painful* past will be as if it never happened. No one will talk or even think about it anymore.

Rev. 21:1-2 (Voice) I looked again *and could hardly believe my eyes*. Everything above me was new. Everything below me was new. *Everything around me was new* because the heaven and earth that had been passed away, and the sea was gone, completely. And I saw the holy city, the new Jerusalem, descending out of heaven from God, prepared like a bride *on her wedding day*, adorned for her husband *and for His eyes only*.

Spaghettification and the Omega-Point

All of our individual and collective identities apart from Christ are being stripped away. Ultimately, as we are drawn forward by the gravity of the New Creation's Omega-point Singularity, we finally start seeing,

CHAPTER 11: IMPARTATION – THE OMEGA-POINT

really *seeing*, that Christ is in all and that Christ **IS** all (see Col 3:11). This awakening happens as we come into the tangible experience of Christ as our Life—as Existence itself.

Any illusions of our alienation from God and each other begin disintegrating on our way toward the Omega-point Singularity. The spaghettification process of peeling back the masks of our body-and-soul false selves continues. Eventually, we will pass through the Singularity, until *everyone* is aware of our interconnected beings, our True Selves—branches on the Christ-vine, waves on the Christ-ocean...ONE.

John 17 paints a beautiful picture of this Oneness when Jesus speaks to the Father about His disciples. This is more than just a wish or dream, as I understood and taught for decades. It's a joyful declaration of God's plan that will culminate in the Omega-point, the inevitable finish toward which our universe is heading.

> **John 17:21-23 (VOICE)** Father, may they all be one as You are in Me and I am in You; may they be in Us, for by this unity the world will believe that You sent Me. All the glory You have given to Me, I pass on to them. May that glory unify them and make them one as We are one, I in them and You in Me, that they may be refined so that all will know that You sent Me, and You love them in the same way You love Me.

This oneness is the reality today, but we are heading into a phase when all will know and embrace and experience it as true; when the knowledge of God's glory covers the earth, like the waters cover the sea. We've seen that the stubborn barrier to embracing this knowledge is the incredibly powerful gravitational pull from our body-and-soul Deepfake avatars, powered by our perceived separation from God and each other. This wicked sense of separation must be spaghettified, exposing our Deepfake images and counterfeit matrix world.

And that's *exactly* what's happening in our world right now.

The world is **not** getting more evil—as I've heard countless people say as they wander around, heads down in hopeless despair. Instead, the exact opposite is true. The world's unreality is being exposed violently as thousands of false identities and fake mindsets of separation make their way to the surface. We are smack dab in the middle of an extended, painful, and repeated spaghettification. The effects of *PoisIF* strains—intricately woven into the entire world-mind system—are being exposed, stripped away, and eliminated. Underneath this painful stripping away lies the Beauty of Christ, emerging as our true identity.

So, please don't forget this larger "Christ-Story" when the chaos around us attempts to distract. The moment we're in now is falling into the infinite gravitational pull of the Omega-point. Christ is filling all things everywhere with Themselves.

> **Rev. 21:6 (AMPC)** And He [further] said to me, "It is done! I am the Alpha and the Omega, the Beginning and the End. To the thirsty I [Myself] will give water without price from the fountain (springs) of the water of Life."

Picture it now! The Great Dance in the pre-Creation Garden will soon go global. What's been taking place within us—our growing awareness that Christ is our only True Identity—will finally be unleashed and expressed phenomenally out in the wide-open fields of lavish grace. We will all fully see, embrace, and celebrate our oneness in Christ!

Second Coming

I'm asked fairly often if our scriptures give us a literal description of a literal arrival of a human-God-representative (Jesus) to set up a literal kingdom. My response: Maybe?! But what if God isn't asking us to relegate this "vision" for some unknown time off in the future? What if They ask us to passionately participate in revealing the essence of that Kingdom here and now? What if Their dream is for us to re-imagine earth—infused with all the elements of heaven that *WE* then confidently express into existence? Maybe, *just maybe,* Christ is waiting to return in a recognizable form *after* we have fulfilled His vision through us for His Good Creation. Perhaps *we* are essentially the second coming of Christ.

As Jesus prayed: Thy Kingdom come,
Thy will be done, on earth
as it is in heaven.

Is this remotely possible, or only a pipe dream? Should we even attempt to imagine it, or is it a waste of our time? If we can't imagine it, we can't step into it. I believe God wants to paint holy images on our soul's whiteboard that erupt and spill into our imagination. Can we picture our

CHAPTER 11: IMPARTATION – THE OMEGA-POINT

holographic, butterfly-effect universe and the all-things-connecting-ocean of the quantum field as our arena in which we, operating from our True Selves, become part of God's vision for Their Good Creation?

Maybe we could phrase it like this, in black hole language: May we confidently join our Christ-Singularities together to create an irresistible gravitational force of Love that calls forth the Reality of God's interconnected world. May any sense of separation from God and each other burn away so that the Reality of Christ would become our tangible, felt identity, as the realm of heaven merges with the earth.

We will forever be drawn further, deeper into the mystery and depths of the eternal Christ. This is where our story is heading, and every moment we operate in the Divine Flow brings us yet another glimpse "on earth, as it is in heaven."

And we will see that this End is actually just a new Beginning.

REFLECTION...Spirit, I'm not always convinced that this Story is going to end well. I know I'm supposed to believe that it will, but I look around the world and see that it's full of horrific hells. Inside my soul, it's often the same. But You are drawing the whole thing forward to a conclusion, which—because it matches Your character—is going to be utterly beautiful...And You're asking me to participate!

My hope and confidence are growing each day. A compelling vision is rising in my imagination, overflowing in ways that help others see Your beauty, our true identity, and the Oneness of the world we inhabit. For all that I don't know and can't know about the future...I trust You.

Collision with Christ: Dream Sequence

A few months after my black hole experience, I had a vivid vision where God reinforced the reality of my *co-crucified co-spaghettified identity* with Them. It was a fitting follow-up to my flight into the Singularity. Since God is never constrained to formulas, Their infinite creativity in revealing Themselves knows no boundaries in how They might communicate this same reality to anyone else. However, I can testify that dreams and visions have been a significant gateway through which God has gotten my attention over the years. This particular dream sequence featured a gap of many months between scenes one and two.

SCENE ONE: I was standing alone on the beach...stretching endlessly to both sides...overlooking a beautiful sunset with brilliant colors donning the horizon. I was soaking it all in. Oh, how I love the ocean!

I recognized some storm clouds starting to brew in the distance, and like dreams sometimes flow, things began to speed up exponentially, and the wind began to whip up the waves as the storm headed my way. I felt the fury of the sky as it drove the ocean into a frenzy, and a vast wall of water started to build and bear down on me in a U-shape pattern. Somehow, I knew that the sky and water's anger was not a random act of nature but directed at me.

As this 40-foot tsunami wave was about to crash on me, I knew without a doubt that the instant it touched me, I was going to die. Then, two things happened in ultra-slow motion the moment before my death...

As the wave froze in time before me:

1. I recognized that it was not water at all. It was raw sewage, filled with the most grotesque, stench-filled substances I had ever known, enough to elicit a vomit reaction (though I held it in). The garbage was moving within the wave like a strange mural, alive and snarling ugly.

2. A flash of understanding came to me. This entire 40-foot wall of sewage, about to end my life, had been entirely generated from within my heart.

Immediately the dream ended.

SCENE TWO: Several months later, during a Sunday service at our church, we were singing a simple chorus during worship time. In an instant, I launched back to the scene on the beach. The wave was about to crush me, and I felt terrified.

Out of the corner of my eye, I saw the blurred image of someone hurtling toward me from the left. I didn't have time to think. I only remember that the eyes were incredibly intense; laser-focused right on me...and I knew that he meant me no harm.

CHAPTER 11: IMPARTATION – THE OMEGA-POINT

I felt the crush of his body hitting me, harder than any linebacker hit I had ever seen, and felt my body driving down into the sand. He buried me completely…I saw only one image before my vision went black, and that was his outstretched body over mine as I fell to the earth, forming the shape of a cross against the background scene.

I felt the weight of the wave crashing down with incredible force but felt none of the pain—for the man who was on me absorbed the raw sewage all into Himself while at the same time absorbing me into Himself. It ended as suddenly as it began, and I launched back to the worship service.

I was left in stunned silence at the gift of this picture, this image of what Christ did to express Their tenacious solidarity with me. It felt crude and raw…intimate and messy and heavy. Somehow, I became part of the cross and the burial…not just figuratively. God did this for me as an explosive way to experience identification with Their Life. And for 100 billion other humans who have existed throughout history, it was just as intense and intimate and heavy. God's "union" with me continued to forge its way into my deepest being, changing from a safe, intellectual concept into something that caused my heart to leap with joy and astonishment. Spaghettification was being reinforced once again through imagery that was personal and vivid.

The raw sewage within me represented the grotesque distortions I had in my mind and heart about God's character. Distortions rooted in my soulish fears and religious anxiety…regrets and what-ifs, disappointments and massive failures…darkness and confusion, and counterfeit thoughts stemming from the unworthiness that separated me from a holy God. But Jesus, the perfect and radiant expression of God's character, absorbed these distortions into Himself as He died.

God is universal and transcendent and also intimate and near. We need to incorporate all of these qualities into our imagination to understand Their true nature. They are the Source of all—the Garden, Creator of the Galaxies…and yet They intimately know every detail of our lives and are always personally present to us.

Even now, no matter how hard I might try, I could never un-see or escape the weight of Love I saw in those piercing eyes…nor would I ever want to. Those eyes…those beautiful eyes.

We have to let this Reality of our union with God soak the inside of us and not remain on our intellectual "nightstand" where we can think about and articulate our ideas from many conceptual angles. This Reality has to explode within us to become a tangible, experiential part of our inner universe. We might describe faith as an effortless inner astonishment when our spirit beholds the reality of Christ. This gives us open access to see that what's true of Them is also true of us. God is the Object and the Source—the Author and Finisher of our faith.

All that is God's by nature is given to us freely as a gift by Their grace.

Gal. 2:20 (KJV) I am crucified with Christ: nevertheless I live; **yet not I, but Christ liveth in me**: and the life which I now live in the flesh **I live by the faith of the Son of God**, who loved me, and gave himself for me.

Chapter 12
Imagination – A Final Fascination
(Post-Revelation)

The word in Hebrew for *paradise* means "an orchard with flowing water." It finds its root in the old Semitic language from the Babylonian culture, meaning "beautiful gardens." From the cross, Jesus told the thief next to Him that he would be with Him that very day in paradise, the same realm that the apostle Paul referred to as the "third heaven" (see 2 Cor. 12:2). It seems like a fitting circle-of-completion that we begin the Story of humanity in a garden and end in one as well.

Third Heaven

The First Heaven is our earth's atmosphere, where birds and clouds share space with us. Beyond this is Second Heaven, where stars live. We call this "space," and the scriptures call this "the heavens," as our pictures from the Hubble telescope confirm. Third Heaven is akin to a place (or dimension) present to all of First and Second Heaven. While it is not ordinarily visible, people do catch a glimpse every so often. In the New Creation, "the heavens will open," and we will see it in full expression as it merges with the earth.

I used to think that "heaven" was a dreamy, ethereal place with angels, clouds, harps, and a throne room where we would attend all-night prayer meetings and participate in a host of extended worship services. This was supposed to be the future that everyone dreamed of, but it sounded kind of boring to me. Later, I thought maybe heaven was a place of perfection, a utopia where we were all on perpetual vacation. But when I stopped to consider this scenario closely, I realized it was also boring. Boring as hell, actually.

I then wondered how a black hole reframe might look...

A Vision for Heaven: Black Hole Reframe

Traditionally, we learned that "heaven" is a place somewhere out in deep space, our hopeful destination eventually in the afterlife. I believe that Jesus paints a different portrait of the heavenly realm *merging* with the earth as we know it today...pictured in Revelation as heaven descending to earth, and God restoring all things.

God is drawing us steadily forward into this ideal "New Heaven and New Earth" environment. Here, our True Selves will have every possible opportunity to learn and grow and express and interact and create—even to heal from the residue and wounds that occurred as our Deepfake selves were stripped away. Time and space won't exist in the way we've known, and the energy field that has been largely conceptual and invisible will be fully accessible for our creative use.

Imagine the unlimited possibilities when we join our unique gifts and passions with others, and express them within the context of deception-free, ego-free relationships that will grow infinitely deeper. What an experience we'll enjoy together as we engage with a universe-filling Garden of Delights!

We can't pretend to know what this New Creation life will be like with any certainty, but it's sure intriguing to consider. I picture that all of us will arrive at the exact same moment, even though our passing from this dimension may occur at different times. What will we find?? Well, we're told in the scriptures to envision a God "greater than anyone can ask or imagine," and I think this is a challenge worth accepting! Since I'm a firm believer that authentic questions are better than pat answers, I figured that ending the book with a series of "ask-or-imagine" questions about the afterlife would be appropriate. Fair enough?!?

- What if we collaborated and designed country-sized theme parks on far off planets and distant galaxies? What kinds of rides and experiences might they include?

CHAPTER 12: IMAGINATION – A FINAL FASCINATION

- With our senses ultra-heightened and super-expanded, what will the music and accompanying choir be like when a billion instruments, two billion voices, and three billion creatures join together with the orchestral sounds of wind, water, fire, and earth to give a universal concert?

- Can we imagine the artists and artwork possible with a palette of 100 trillion trillion colors and no limit to the type of elements we can access and use as art forms, obtained from across the universe?

- What will it look like to share our stories' details and see the near-infinite ways our earthly existence has overlapped with billions of others and prepared us for our experience in the New Creation?

- What will it look like to represent our individual and collective stories artistically and mathematically inside an interactive holographic sphere the size of Jupiter?

- Since time will be a sliding scale, what if every version of our earth-selves is present in a tangible form so that we can hang out with/as past and future versions of ourselves and others in places that are meaningful in our history? Imagine the extraordinary meals and experiences and healing we might enjoy as we have these magnificent conversations?

- Will we be able to imagine things into being? What would these be if we are motivated by our True Selves, operating with a desire for increased wholeness, vibrancy, creativity, wisdom, experience, joy, intimacy, education, curiosity, authenticity?

- Can we celebrate each person who ever lived for their unique Christ-expression? Not just for the spectacular things they've done, but for the specific facet of the whole that their magnificent life embodies, without which the Story would be incomplete? Maybe we should take the equivalent of eleven earth-years per person for this universe-wide celebration?

- What if everyone had meaningful work, doing what they loved, and their work was necessary to the New Creation's ongoing sustenance and health? Will this be mixed with marvelous forms of play and baby-like rest?

INTO THE ABYSS

- Could there still be the possibility to experience pain and conflict and violence, and restoration and healing and forgiveness?

- Can we interact with the earth, especially plant and animal kingdoms, in meaningful, symbiotic ways that help us see and understand their place in the Story? Will some of us have dragons and dinosaurs as pets?

- Is it possible to have sports and games that allow for the full display of physical and mental skills, absent any negative dynamics, while keeping the sheer thrill of excitement and healthy competition?

- Will we teleport instantly to various jaw-dropping landscapes in other continents, or on Jupiter, or a few million light-years past Andromeda, etc....then watch and listen as their atomic frequencies become a language to communicate the beauty of how they came into being?

- Can we choose to temporarily "trade" our awareness and consciousness with others, to experience their life events leading them to this point?

- What if we could fully enter into our dreams and seamlessly pull out key elements into the New Creation? What if boundaries between the dream world and the Real World were easily traversed?

- Can we insert ourselves into a subatomic particle, perhaps a photon, and re-live its experience from the Creation until now? Can this experience come with a full range of sensations, so we get the total immersion into their "universe" as if it were ours?

- Will we meet advanced forms of life from other planets, galaxies, and universes that help fill in missing pieces from our human history on earth?

- Would we be surprised if our earthly stories were a part of God's "holy scriptures," and each one of us had a book inside of this sacred library?

- Will we discover that God has collected every tear we've ever cried, combined it with Their own, and used it to water and nourish our inner soul-garden through the course of our lives?

CHAPTER 12: IMAGINATION – A FINAL FASCINATION

- How will sexual intimacy be a part of our relationships, perhaps reimagined? What if we will feel the pleasure and sensations of sex in creative ways, with no shame or regret, where spirit and soul intimacy is so deep and pure that it overflows into the physical realm?

- Will there be classes, workshops, tours, retreats, and immersive experiences led by giants in their fields of expertise, that we can join to continue learning eternally about all there is to know? Maybe each of us has, or will have, something of great value to bring to these discussions?

- Perhaps God will take on a recognizable form and make Their way to each of us, holding our gaze until we are **known** unlike we've ever been known before? Will we experience the delight and adoration of our Source in a personal, intimate form that explodes within us into the full experience of what it means to be a Divine image-bearing human?

There won't be anything remotely static, predictable, routine, or boring about this existence. With our senses sharpened and expanded to absorb and process incredible ranges of inputs, and our souls humming along in harmony with our spirit, we will truly be able to explore the full range of the human experience. We'll be learning and growing, expressing and creating, fostering new ways of relating and interacting—eternally!

It turns out this "ending" is simply a New Beginning. And we'll remember that every time the love of Christ overflowed through us in our lives, we manifested a glimmering glimpse of this reality and took yet one more necessary step in merging the Real World with the Matrix...the Third Heaven with our current earth. We will be drawn ever deeper into the depths of an infinitely expanding beautiful existence as we mirror our infinite God.

Oasis for the Soul

It does our soul a heap of good to meditate on these things—not just for a few hurried minutes before rushing off to start our to-do lists, or pursuing the next new insight-of-the-month...These realities must make their way down deep in our soul, slowly and deliberately. As we take our regular 11-second breaths in solitude and silence, we give our soul the space to open wide and digest seeds of Divine life, eternal seeds of possibility that long to burst forth from the depths of our inner universe. Christ is baptizing us, immersing us into Their eternal Story, and leading all of humanity to the holy, universal celebration of our Divine Union.

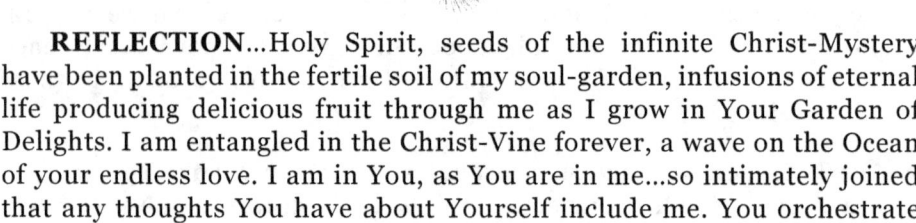

REFLECTION...Holy Spirit, seeds of the infinite Christ-Mystery have been planted in the fertile soil of my soul-garden, infusions of eternal life producing delicious fruit through me as I grow in Your Garden of Delights. I am entangled in the Christ-Vine forever, a wave on the Ocean of your endless love. I am in You, as You are in me...so intimately joined that any thoughts You have about Yourself include me. You orchestrate clues across the Cosmos that declare these mind-bending realities, spoken in languages that resonate with my inner being. The exploration of Your Creation draws my heart and mind to awestruck wonder, and I am eternally grateful.

I sense Your delight as You celebrate my existence amid ongoing chaos in and around me. Thank You for my uncreated, unchanging spirit—Your breath-print—that defines my core being, the essence of my true identity. My gratitude bursts from deep within me like nuclear fusion as I remember my eternal place in Your Divine Sanctuary...my unique role in the steady unfolding of Your beautiful Story. Remind me, remind us all that we are full-time, lifetime incarnations of Christ—the Magnificent Love that creates and unites and sustains all that exists.

CHAPTER 12: IMAGINATION – A FINAL FASCINATION

The Ludicrous Lover

The Universe knew of you long before time,
  Long before creatures, contagions and crime.
    Way before anything ever existed,
    You were the DREAM of a Love that consisted
  Of Beauty and Passion and Freedom and Grace,
Of Laughter and Joy at the thought of your face.

You melted the heart
  Of a Ludicrous Lover,
    Fanatical Friend —
      You, Their gem to uncover.

You came into being, a child of the Light
  But darkness swept in and your soul felt its fright
    The freaks and the frizzles, they frazzled your soul,
      The shrieks and the shrizzles, they swallowed you whole.

    But Love is a Warrior, and you were Its prize
    Love raged against darkness, deception, and lies
  Explosion of Light, left a glow that persisted
The ocean of night simply could not resist it.

As Light floods your eyes, Love can show you its scope,
  Of healing and wholeness and heavenly hope . . .

The Ludicrous Lover,
  Awaits now a chance,
    Their eyes bid you come
      To be part of The Dance.

INTO THE ABYSS

Black Hole Theology: An 11-point Summary of the Christ Story

1. Christ is the Alpha-point Singularity in Whom the entire Cosmos existed before the Creation. (John 1:2-4, Col. 1:15-17)

2. On the other side of Creation's black hole—the Christ-Singularity—is God's reality, eternally existing as a Divine flow of love, marked by a beautiful, intimate relationship within the Holy Sanctuary. (Gen. 1:26, John 17:22-24)

3. The Lamb slain from before the world's foundation is a picture of God's essence—unconditional eternal love for all—which included us in the Divine Life via our co-crucifixion with Christ. This demonstrates the process of spaghettification required to strip away the false identities that have attached themselves to us over time. (2 Cor. 5:14-19, Gal. 2:20, 1 Pet. 1:20, Rev. 13:8)

4. Our True Selves existed in God before the Creation, the realm of our true identity eternally joined with Christ. (Eph. 1:4)

5. Christ created everything, and everyone in the Cosmos. It all remains connected, held together, and sustained in Christ. This interconnected reality of our existence is called the Kingdom of heaven (Jesus' words) and the quantum field (scientific language). (Col. 1:15-17, Luke 17:21)

6. Separation from God is only in our minds. In reality, such separation is impossible because we cannot be separated from the very Source and Sustenance of our existence. (Job 33:4, Rom. 8:38-39, Acts 17:28)

7. The great lie that says sin separated us from a holy God has been planted like a deadly poison into humanity's soul-garden, fostering an environment where we ran and hid in fear and shame. This led to us pursuing counterfeit identity and purpose (our Deepfake false selves) apart from the loving affirmation overflowing within the Divine sanctuary. (Gen 3:7-13)

8. Humanity's sordid history is filled with the effects of believing this separation-lie (from God and each other). It brought disharmony, confusion, violence, and darkness to the human race. (Rom. 1:25)

9. Jesus came to demolish the lie of our separation from God and remind us of our Divine Origin in Christ, of God's unconditional love for the whole world, and of our union with the Divine that shapes our true identity and purpose. (Rom. 5:18, 2 Cor. 5:19, Eph. 3:8-11, Eph. 4:6, Col. 1:19-22)

CHAPTER 12: IMAGINATION – A FINAL FASCINATION

10. We each have unique and necessary roles (full-time, lifetime expressions of Christ that flow from our true identity) in the eternal story of God. We must see the world with new childlike eyes to manifest heaven's reality into the earth realm. Our thoughts, emotions, and intentions are seeds of possibility, locally expressed into the quantum field's holographic reality, and carry eternal influence on the whole. (Ps. 139:13-18, Matt. 6:10, Eph. 2:10, Col. 3:3)

11. Christ is the Omega-point Singularity that continuously restores all things through us (*apokatastasis*) and draws the whole Cosmos forward to the New Creation. (Isa. 65:17, Acts 3:20-21, Rev. 21:5-6)

On the last weekend in January 2006, I gave up on my Christianity. Fortunately, God...*They*...never gave up on me. What emerged in place of my self-righteous religious certainty is more beautiful and life-giving than I could have ever imagined, especially looking back at the early stages of deconstruction when I wasn't sure my faith would survive. The Oasis of Truth I had been fiercely chasing all my life had been inside me the whole time, immersing me, pursuing me all along.

I just didn't know it...but now, *in this moment*, I do.

I imagine with joyful confidence, the jaw-dropping experience all of us will have as we come to know the reality of Christ as our True Identity, and I ask God that our lives become Light-mirrors of this Love that resides at the heart of the universe. I believe we'll eventually discover that all of our childlike explorations are leading us one steady step at a time toward the explosive, life-altering awareness of Christ—Our Source and Sustainer and Harmony—the True Reality, *filling everything everywhere* with Themselves. Oneness.

Each one of us has a role in the beautiful unfolding
of God's Eternal Story.
Dive deep.

I trust that the portrait of Christ I've attempted to paint points to a Beauty

far greater than my thoughts and words

are able to convey.

In Their Love,

Influences in Writing This Book

The following are my **"Top 10" recommended books** to help navigate the de/re-construction of a faith journey, especially for those who come from an evangelical Christian tradition like mine, and are now perhaps curious about exploring perspectives different from the ones you have likely been taught.

*Brad Jersak, *A More Christlike God*, CWR Press; April 22, 2015, 1st ed. (Note: The heart of a pastor, and the insight of a theologian, clearly articulating a vision of Jesus as the perfect exegesis of God's character)

*Brian Zahnd, *Sinners in the Hands of a Loving God*, WaterBrook, August 15, 2017. (Note: Jonathan Edwards' famous sermon gets a serious reframe in this excellent theological treatment of how God's love shapes our worldview)

*William P. Young, *The Shack*, Windblown Media, June 20, 2008. *(Note:* Still one of the best novels I've ever read, about the deep healing that takes place within a man who encounters God in an abandoned shack in the woods)

*C. Baxter Kruger, *The Undoing of Adam*, Perichoresis Press, August 9, 2011. (Note: Baxter's story-telling is second to none, and here he paints a picture of Jesus as Second Adam and His effect on the entire human race)

*Richard Rohr, *Immortal Diamond*, Jossey-Bass; January 2, 2012, 1st ed. (Note: This masterful book shows us how to uncover the diamond of our True Self amidst the debris and junk of our False Self)

*Peter Enns, *The Bible Tells Me So*, HarperOne; September 9, 2014, reprint ed. (Note: This scholarly work is a must-read for any who want to take the Bible seriously, in context, and learn to see it for what it actually is)

INTO THE ABYSS

*Ilaria Ramelli, *Apokatastasis*, BRILL August 9, 2013. (Note: It's expensive, but this book is the most complete and thoroughly researched work on apokatastasis that I'm aware exists; there is a condensed version available)

*Brennan Manning, *Abba's Child*, Navpress 1997. (Note: On the topic of Grace, I recommend the heartfelt and tender works of Brennan Manning and the provocative but profound works of Robert F. Capon)

*David Bentley Hart, *That All Shall Be Saved*, Yale University Press, September 24, 2019. (Note: The snark is heavy in this one, and so is his traditional affection for big words, but it's a powerful treatment of ultimate reconciliation by a renowned Eastern Orthodox scholar)

*Rachel Held Evans, *Searching for Sunday*, Thomas Nelson, April 14, 2015. (Note: This beautifully written work highlights a compelling vision of what it means to be part of the Church, separate from cheap platitudes)

Additional Theological Influences: For Further Exploration

Note: The resources below were all significant at some point along my spiritual journey, and I am grateful for their experiences that formed a trail of "bread crumbs" leading to my own Spirit-guided exploration…

Books

Rob Bell, *Velvet Elvis*, Collins 2012.

Sadhu Sundar Singh, *At the Master's Feet*, Signalman Publishing, June 1, 2008.

Michael Hardin, *Jesus Driven Life*, JDL Press; September 26, 2013, 2nd ed.

Jeff Turner, *Atheistic Theist*, Jeff Turner; November 20, 2016, 1st ed.

Francois Du Toit, *The Mirror Bible*, Mirrorword Publishing; August 1, 2018, revised ed.

Greg Boyd, *Crucifixion of the Warrior God*, Fortress Press; April 17, 2017, combined ed.

Diana Butler Bass, *Grounded*, HarperOne; October 6, 2015, reprint ed.

Richard Rohr, *The Universal Christ*, SPCK Publishing, March 5, 2019.

Bakht Singh, (various booklets), Gospel Literature Service, 1964.

Jim Palmer, *Notes from (Over) the Edge*, Divine Nobodies Press, November 30, 2013.

Robert F. Capon, *Kingdom Grace Judgment*, Eerdmans; March 11, 2002, combined ed.

Origen, *On First Principles*, Christian Classics, December 9, 2013.

Teresa of Avila, *The Interior Castle*, Dover Publications, December 17, 2007.

St John of the Cross, *Dark Night of the Soul*, Dover Publications, March 6, 2012.

INTO THE ABYSS

C.S. Lewis, (Chronicles of Narnia) *The Last Battle*, HarperCollins, 2000.

Watchman Nee, *Release of the Spirit*, Living Stream Ministry; June 1, 1997, Later Printing ed.

Karl Barth, *Church Dogmatics An Intro and Reader*, T&T Clark; December 18, 2012, 1st ed.

George MacDonald, *Unspoken Sermons*, Start Publishing LLC, November 26, 2012.

St Catherine of Sienna, *letter 368 to Stefano Maconi*.

Additional Scientific Influences: For Further Exploration

Note: I used the resources below to shape and clarify some of the scientific and philosophical content in my book, though they aren't quoted directly. It was also a thrill this year as I was finishing this book to learn that three scientists who cemented the *reality of black holes* were jointly awarded the Nobel Prize in physics, as announced by the Royal Swedish Academy of Sciences on October 6, 2020.

Books

Hawking, Stephen, *A Brief History of Time*, New York: Bantam Books, 1998.

Braden, Gregg, *The Divine Matrix*, Carlsbad, Calif: Hay House, 2007.

Campbell, Joseph, Cousineau, Phil. The Hero's Journey: Joseph Campbell On His Life And Work; Collected Works Of Joseph Campbell. Shaftesbury, Element, 1999.

Girard, Rene, *Things Hidden since the Foundation of the World*, Research undertaken in collaboration with Jean-Michel Oughourlian and Guy Lefort. Stanford, CA: Stanford University Press, 1987.

Greene, Brian, *The Elegant Universe*, W. W. Norton & Co., Oct 11, 2010, 2nd ed.

Heisenberg, Werner. "Ordnung der Wirklichkeit" ("Reality and Its Order"), published in *Collected Works. Section C: Philosophical and Popular Writings. Volume I. Physics and Cognition. 1927-1955* (1984).

Heisenberg, Werner. *Das Naturgesetz und die Struktur der Materie* (1967), as translated in *Natural Law and the Structure of Matter* (1981).

Petersen, Jordan, *12 Rules for Life*, Random House Canada; January, 2018.

Ravelli, Carlo, *7 Brief Lessons on Physics,* Riverhead Books, March 1, 2016.

Ross, Hugh, *Creation and Time*, Orlando, FL: Signalman Publishing, 2010, 3rd ed.

Tyson, Neil D., *Astrophysics for People in a Hurry*, W.W. Norton & Company, 2017.

Yee, Jeff, *The Particles of the Universe*, Copyright Jan 2018, 12th ed.

Websites

Hubble Telescope	https://hubblesite.org/
Event Horizon Telescope	https://eventhorizontelescope.org/
Energy Wave Equations	https://energywavetheory.com/
BioLogos	https://biologos.org/
Pierre Tielhard De Chardin	http://teilharddechardin.org/

Poetic Influences:
For Further Enjoyment

Note: These artists have significantly shaped the way I see the world over the past few decades, and you'll see hints of their influence sprinkled throughout the book. In unique, delightful ways, these poets express the Beauty that I wrote about in the introduction; the very kind of Beauty that has the power to transform our world.

Theodor S. Geisel (Dr. Seuss)

Jalāl ad-Dīn Muhammad Rumi (Rumi)

Khwāja Shams-ud-Dīn Muḥammad Ḥāfeẓ-e Shīrāzī (Hafiz)

Mary Oliver

e.e. cummings

John Donahue

Robindronath Thakur (Tagore)

Emily Dickinson

Rainer Maria Rilke

Maya Angelou

About the Author

When Mo was in 4th grade, his teacher put his essay titled "Dr. Von Bunsen-burner" on the wall as an example of good creative writing. A subtle seed was planted that day! Many decades later, he encountered the same Muse and began journaling daily...eventually, those entries, along with extended time in front of a whiteboard, would form the content for this book.

Mo has been told on numerous occasions that he should stick with crashing cars for the auto industry (which he's done for 30 years in the Detroit, MI area), instead of attempting to write about theology. This seems like good advice, as he has no seminary degree, limited ministry experience, no impressive titles that lend any credibility...and engineers aren't often known for their writing.

He decided to write this book anyway. In fact, NOT writing it wasn't an option...His sincere hope is for readers to experience a taste of the Delicious Beauty of Christ that's been marinating the universe for billions of years.

Join the ongoing conversation on Mo's Facebook page, which often swirls around the themes in this book.

More from Eyes Open Press

Eyes Open Press is a unique publishing house with a vision to sound loud the trumpet of God's all-encompassing grace. If you enjoyed Into the Abyss, check out Dylan DeMarisco's The Happy Trinity or Nick Padovani's The Song of the Ages. Both are available at Amazon and at www.eyesopenpress.com.

To see more of Mo's writings, as well as authors with a similar vision, check out the online magazine Elisha's Riddle. This publication is a monthly dose of wonder and revelation, along with a hope-filled view of the future. Each subscription supports the work of Eyes Open Press in helping authors and creators release the Good News!

 Discover more at www.ElishasRiddle.com